C000181306

THE LOPAPEYSA SWEATER

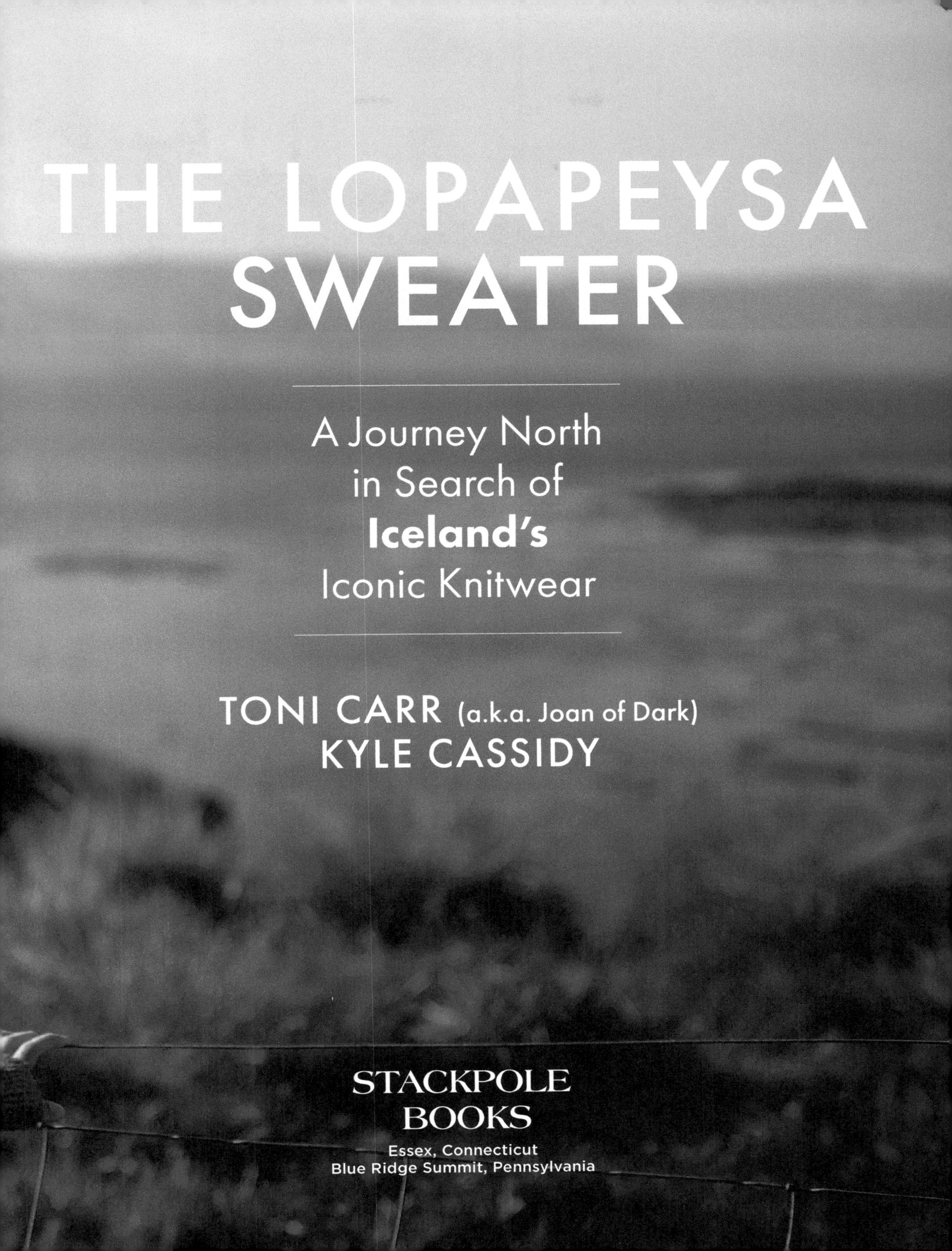

THE LOPAPEYSA SWEATER

A Journey North
in Search of
Iceland's
Iconic Knitwear

TONI CARR (a.k.a. Joan of Dark)
KYLE CASSIDY

**STACKPOLE
BOOKS**

Essex, Connecticut
Blue Ridge Summit, Pennsylvania

STACKPOLE BOOKS

An imprint of Globe Pequot, the trade division of The Rowman & Littlefield Publishing Group, Inc.
4501 Forbes Blvd., Ste. 200
Lanham, MD 20706
www.rowman.com

Distributed by NATIONAL BOOK NETWORK
800-462-6420

Copyright © 2022 Toni Carr, Kyle Cassidy
Knitting instructions and patterns: Toni Carr (a.k.a. Joan of Dark)
Photography and travel chapters: Kyle Cassidy

Schematics:
Zabet Groznaya
Dan Carr
Lisa Conway

Tech editing:
Lisa Conway
Laura Hohman
Brambles and Bindweed TE
Kerry Bullock-Ozkan

All rights reserved. No part of this book may be reproduced in any form or by any electronic or mechanical means, including information storage and retrieval systems, without written permission from the publisher, except by a reviewer who may quote passages in a review.

The contents of this book are for personal use only. Patterns herein may be reproduced in limited quantities for such use. Any large-scale commercial reproduction is prohibited without the written consent of the publisher.

We have made every effort to ensure the accuracy and completeness of these instructions. We cannot, however, be responsible for human error, typographical mistakes, or variations in individual work.

British Library Cataloguing in Publication Information available

Library of Congress Cataloging-in-Publication Data available

ISBN 978-0-8117-3983-2 (paper : alk. paper)
ISBN 978-0-8117-6976-1 (electronic)

♾™ The paper used in this publication meets the minimum requirements of American National Standard for Information Sciences—Permanence of Paper for Printed Library Materials, ANSI/ NISO Z39.48-1992.

First Edition

For Pálína Gunnarsdóttir, Hera Hjartardottir, Guðlaug Berglind Björnsdottir, Rebekka Guðleifsdóttir, Margrét Þórdís, Anna Halla, Védís Jónsdóttir, and all the Icelandic knitters who have been a part of this tradition and shared their stories, history, and wisdom with us.

A travel adventure for knitters and the people who love them.

Contents

Note: Travel chapters are by Kyle Cassidy.
Knitting instructions and patterns are by Toni Carr (a.k.a. Joan of Dark).

Kyle and Joan behind the scenes at Jökulsárlón Glacier Lagoon. Photo by Trillian Stars.

Introduction

This is no ordinary knitting book. However much fun reading a knitting book is, *making* one can be a thousand times better.

The last book that we did together, *Geek Knits*, turned out to be an incredible and life-changing adventure. We spent a year with people from *Star Trek*, *Game of Thrones*, *Robot Chicken*, and *Mystery Science Theater 3000* and with coroners, engineers, and punk rockers. We stayed with horror director John Carpenter and his wife, comic and movie producer Sandy King, in Hollywood. We crashed on Neil Gaiman's sofas, stayed in George R. R. Martin's guesthouse, and spent an evening in the Mythbusters Mancave. We walked in the woods with US Women's Chess champion Jennifer Shahade, went jogging with novelist John Scalzi and his wife, Krissy (OK, John cheered from afar while the rest of us jogged), and spent time with so many amazing people. Writing the book was so much fun that we started looking for ways that we could share that experience with people again,

the next time we did a book—and Iceland was perfect for that.

What you have in your hands is not just a knitting book; it's the story of how a knitting book gets made: finding the inspiration, learning about the history and the industry, picking up the stitches. It's the behind-the-scenes research, the travel, and the photography that makes a knitting book happen. In short, it was an amazing, life-changing experience, and *you* should have an amazing, life-changing experience too.

Iceland is the perfect place for knitters and the people who love them to visit together. Next to every yarn shop is a spectacular waterfall, farm, café, hot spring, or glacier; craft breweries dot the volcanic landscape, and there is no vista that isn't breathtaking. Pack your needles, your tent, and someone you love, and spend some time in the land of ice and fire knitting and, just as importantly, *not* knitting. You won't regret it.

Kyle and Joan

It's Easy to Get to Iceland. You Should Go.

Iceland may seem very remote, and for a long time it really was. The city of Reykjavik, for example, on the southwest coast, is at latitude 64° north—which is 1,650 miles *north* of New York City. That's the equivalent of getting in your car and driving north from Manhattan at 55 mph (80 kmh) until you fall off the top of Canada 30 hours later. And then you'd *still* have 200 miles (322 km) to go before you hit latitude 64° north—which would be at Cape Dorset on Baffin Island. That's near where Sir John Franklin's 1845 search for the Northwest Passage failed miserably: his ships froze in the ice and were crushed to bits because it's so freaking cold up there. But Iceland, though it *is* that far north, *isn't* actually that cold. They can have some miserable winters, for sure, but Iceland also sits at the top of the Gulf Stream, which brings warm water and air up from Central America straight to the island— so the temperatures are typically warmer in the summer than other places at the same latitude.[1]

The story about the Vikings naming the warm, hospitable island Iceland and the frozen, inhospitable one Greenland in order to discourage tourists isn't true, but Iceland is mostly a lot easier to get to and get around in and has better weather than you might expect. As for its remoteness, for Americans and anybody in the European Union, Iceland is actually pretty easy to get to—it's a four-hour flight from New York or Boston, you don't need a visa, and, after an aggressive campaign by Icelandair starting in 2010, there are flights from throughout the United States. By 2016, the number of American tourists in Iceland exceeded the number of native Icelanders for the first time. And by 2020, tourists could sometimes outnumber natives by as much as six to one.[2]

Once you get to the Land of Ice and Fire, though, it's not cheap. In fact, since it's an island and everything needs to be shipped to it, Iceland is the most expensive country in Europe. But there are things you can do to keep costs down, like shopping for food at the grocery store rather than eating out, staying at one of the many Airbnbs instead of hotels, and bringing things in with you. (At the moment, Iceland allows every person to bring 6.6 pounds [3 kg] of food with them and

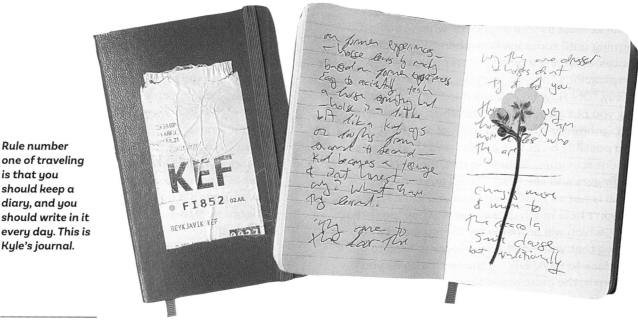

Rule number one of traveling is that you should keep a diary, and you should write in it every day. This is Kyle's journal.

---

1. The average January temperature in Reykjavik is between three degrees above freezing to two degrees below freezing, while in New York City (1,600 miles to the south), the average temperature is between four degrees above freezing to three degrees below freezing. Temperature averages taken from https://www.timeanddate.com/weather/usa/new-york/climate.
2. https://www.travelandleisure.com/trip-ideas/iceland-american-tourists.

Currency

Although Iceland is part of the European Union, it doesn't use the euro. It has its own money, the Icelandic króna (abbreviated ISK). It's the second-smallest country in the world to have its own currency (the first is the Republic of Seychelles, a chain of 115 islands in the Indian Ocean, which has less than 100,000 citizens). Króna means "crown" and is derived from the Danish *krone* (also "crown") because, for a long and complex time, Iceland was part of Denmark (this relationship is explained in a mural along the wall of the airport on the way to Customs, so if you're stuck in line, you can learn more about it there). Obviously, check conversion rates before you go, but the króna is worth about (waves hand) a penny. One way to ballpark the cost of something is to put your thumb over the last two digits of a price and pretend it's in dollars. So a lovely sweater that's selling for 24,000 ISK is *about* $240 (as of this writing, it's actually $193, but overestimating the cost will keep you from having a heart attack when you get home and figure out what you spent for a sandwich).

1.5 liters of liquor.[3] You should absolutely do this.) Aside from the easy travel and plentiful accommodations, most younger people speak English at least as well as you do, which you find charming until someone is rambling along for ten minutes, dropping words like "crepuscular" and "perspicacious," only to stumble at some point and say, "Oh! How do you say it in English? The thing you put on your foot?" to which you will first grunt ignorantly—unable to think of anything that could possibly be put on a foot—and then after a moment stammer, "Shoe?" At this, they will snap their fingers and say, "Yes! Shoe! I am sorry, my English is not so good." And then you'll just be sad and won't hear much of the rest of what they are saying, which will probably be something about America that you didn't know. Tourists tend to stick close to Reykjavik, so the farther away you get from it, the more alone time you'll have with the locals.

Pronunciation

Icelandic is very difficult to pronounce for Americans. Resign yourself to the fact that you're going to get it wrong, but if you can get close enough, Icelanders will nod politely, assume you suffered brain damage as a child, and point you to your destination. Here's a quick pronunciation guide:

- Most consonants are pronounced similarly to English.
- Accent marks usually function like doubling the vowel would in English.
- *A* is pronounced as it is in *far*, but *Á* is ow(!)—like you stubbed your toe.
- *I* and *Y* and *Í* and *Ý* are exactly the same; they just accent some of them to make it difficult for you to type Icelandic words.
- *E* is pronounced as in *meh*; but with an accent, *É* is like the first half of an exasperated *yeah*—think of the sound you would make if someone asked you if you understood Icelandic pronunciations.
- An *F* functions either like an *F* or a *V*, and although there are rules, it's basically a coin toss. Schoolteachers in Iceland tell students that most Icelandic rules have more exceptions than applicable cases.
- *Ei, Ey* you'll see often, and they both make a long *a* sound.
- *Æ* is the letter "ash" and is pronounced exactly like *ey*. In fact, when Gen Z Icelanders are texting one another and making fun of English (it happens), they substitute *Æ* for "I," as in "Æ þeink jú verí mutsj for jor gúd companí!"
- *Hv* shows up a lot, and is pronounced *kv*, like "kvetch."
- *J* is pronounced like *y*.
- *Ll*—two *Ls* together are pronounced with a *tl* sound, as in "little."
- *Ö* makes a sound like the *ur* in "urn." So "Motörhead" should actually be pronounced "Mo-tur-head."
- *R* is rolled.
- *Þ, þ* is the character "thorn" like *th* in "the."
- *Ð, ð* is the character "eth" and it also makes a *th* sound, like *th* in "think."

---

3. In this book we're using both the metric and the imperial systems of measurement. I didn't do it here, though, because you already know what a liter is—it's like a quart. And this will really trip you up when you go to buy gasoline, because it's sold by the liter, and it's like ten times more expensive than you think it could possibly be. So your mind will first try to tell you that the sign must mean gallons and that it must also be wrong, because no way on earth could a gallon of gas be that expensive—and yet it can and it is.

Iceland's History of Wool

Sheep were introduced to Iceland by the Vikings during the Middle Ages, and because Iceland is an island, the sheep have developed as a unique breed, unknown anywhere else in the world. These sheep have a double-coated fleece that both insulates them and keeps them dry. There is a long, coarse, wiry outer coat fiber called the *tog*, which has water-repellent properties, and a warm, insulating inner coat called the *thel* (*þel*). When the two coats are used together, they make *lopi*, and together they give Icelandic wool the unique characteristics that make it ideal in cold, wet weather *and* that allow it to be knit unspun. While typically used to represent "Icelandic wool" in its totality, the word *lopi* actually means "roving" in Icelandic—roving is a band of loosely connected fiber ready to be made into yarn on a spinning wheel (don't feel bad, most Icelanders don't know this). In 1923, a woman named Elín Guðmundsdóttir Snæhólm wrote in the magazine *Hlín* that she was able to successfully use lopi in a sock-knitting machine to make a scarf.[1] The chief value of knitting unspun fibers was speed—if you could skip the spinning process, you could get products to market more quickly.

In her 1985 book, *Women's Work in Iceland for 1100 Years*, Anna Sigurðardóttir wrote that while Snæhólm was the first to publish about knitting with lopi, she wasn't the first to actually do it. Two women from Mýrasýsla, Margrét Sigurðardóttir and Gunnvör Magnúsdóttir, successfully knit unspun wool by hand during the "great frost" of 1917–1918, when the weather caught them unprepared for a sudden need for more mittens and scarves. They kept their discovery a secret, though, embarrassed by their unpreparedness.[2]

Icelandic sheep come in 17 different natural colors, a quality that helps make them popular with knitters. They were popular with the Vikings for other reasons, chief among them being that when it was too cold to plant vegetables, you could occasionally eat one of your sheep. According to the Department of Animal Sciences at Ohio State University, where they study this stuff, Icelandic sheep, while they have great wool, are primarily raised for meat, and only about 20 percent of a farmer's money comes from fleece.

1. Elín Kr. Guðmundsdóttir Snæhólm, "Sneis, Laxárdal, Húnavatnssýslu: Að spara spunann," *Hlín* 7 (1923): 40–41.
2. Anna Sigurðardóttir, *Women's Work in Iceland for 1100 Years* (*Vinna kvenna á Íslandi í 1100 ár*), 1985, 360.

When you get to a wool store in Iceland, you'll find lopi, either unspun or lightly spun, in a variety of weights:

- *Plötulopi.* Completely unspun wool that comes in plates. People will often take the outside end and the center end and knit with these together. This is the most authentic way to knit your sweater, but it's not convenient.
- *Einband.* A single, finespun thread for lace knitting made only from þel, the soft undercoat; it's also commonly knitted held next to a strand of plötulopi.
- *Léttlopi.* Made of two strands of plötulopi.
- *Álafoss.* Worsted weight equivalent to three strands of plötulopi.
- *Jöklalopi.* A bulky yarn (formerly called *bulkylopi*, not kidding) that's twice as thick as álafoss. Use it for chunky sweaters, mittens, hats, and blankets.
- *Hosuband.* A worsted weight that's reinforced with nylon to make it more resilient.

Álafoss was the major company behind Icelandic yarn from the late 1800s until it went bankrupt in 1991 and was bought out by a consortium of former employees and farmers who created Ístex from its ashes. Ístex now produces most of the wool in Iceland, and if you've bought lopi yarn in the United States, it's probably come from Ístex.

Icelandic Wool in the United States

Icelandic wool was imported into the United States for quite some time before it became popular in fashion. Things changed for a time in the mid-20th century, when a process was developed that allowed the tog to be separated and the soft þel to be sold alone, for a while, as a less expensive alternative to merino. Today, the vast majority of Icelandic wool is sold unseparated. Much of the history of the lopapeysa is the history of Iceland—and the world—coming to love the pragmatism of the lopi wool as it is: rugged and functional.

The wool was a boon to the Vikings, allowing them to move into the Secondary Products Revolution, transitioning from wearing primary animal products—for example, furs—to secondary products such as wool. The wool was good, but the sheep were a menace and proceeded to eat every green thing on the island, destroying all of the native trees, denuding the landscape, and causing devastating soil erosion, which is still a problem to this day.

About the Lopapeysa

The lopapeysa (or lopi for short) is the iconic Icelandic sweater, but what is that? *Lopapeysa* means "Icelandic wool jumper," and *jumper* means "sweater."[1] The lopi sweater is unique in the world not just because of its patterns but also because of the very distinctive wool. You may ask, *"Is a sweater with a traditional Icelandic patterned yoke knitted out of acrylic still a lopi?"* Most Icelanders who would care to argue would likely argue, *"No, it's not."* And to get the real experience, you really should knit your sweater with Icelandic wool. That's not stopping companies in Iceland and elsewhere from mass-producing and selling tourists all sorts of sweaters made out of decidedly not Icelandic wool.

Icelandic scholar, fiber expert, and author of *Icelandic Lopi Sweater: Origin, History and Design* Ásdís Jóelsdóttir provided us with a succinct definition when we asked her: "The Icelandic lopi sweater is made from unspun Icelandic wool (lopi) in natural colors and knitted on circular needles, with a band of pattern around the yoke and a section of the pattern repeated around the lower part of the body and the end of the sleeves."

Taking this as a starting point, a lot of creative knitters have played with, added, and subtracted from that definition to produce an ever-varying, living design that can change with the times but also pays homage to the originals.

The lopapeysa is ubiquitous in Iceland. It's not just a tourist thing: nearly everyone in Iceland has at least one lopi with a story behind it. There is really no American equivalent. But the history of this national treasure is a bit of a mystery. Nobody's exactly sure where or when it appeared, but most historians who've dug deep into it agree that it was a lot more recently than we'd think.

In her 2009 paper "Nation in a Sheep's Coat: The Icelandic Sweater," Guðrun Helgadóttir, PhD, called the Icelandic sweater an "invented tradition":

The Icelandic sweater as we now know it emerged around the middle of the 20th century and was influenced, on one hand, by the nature of the material used and, on the other hand, by folk patterns of neighboring nations. The sweater soon became so popular that in my childhood, during the 60s and 70s, one might say that the sweater was the Icelander's uniform or vernacular national dress. The Icelandic sweater was in tune with the times: it was handmade from natural fiber, it had folk connotations, and almost every Icelandic woman could knit one.[2]

It's as though the lopi sprang fully formed from the forehead of 1950s Iceland and quickly became a symbol of the country and a point of pride. Have I said that there's nothing like it in America?

One mesmerizing clue to the lopapeysa's origins is a 1998 interview with Auður Laxness by Anna Kristine Magnúsdóttir in *Vikan* magazine, where Auður claims to have been the inventor of the lopi. Auður was the wife of writer Halldór Laxness and a major force in the preservation of Icelandic culture. In the interview, she says that Halldór, while visiting South America in the 1950s, brought her back a book about Inca patterns and, inspired by this, she knit what became the lopapeysa.[3] One thing that we were interested in finding out during our trip was whether that was true.

The lopi has become intrinsically interwoven with Iceland's personal identity. Designer and *Lopi* book editor Védís Jónsdóttir has said that to Icelanders the lopi is "like a flag."[4] This is well borne out. In 2016, Icelandair celebrated the beginning of its nonstop flights to and from Chicago by dispatching Icelandic minister of industry and commerce Ragnheiður Elín Árnadóttir to give the mayor, Rahm Emanuel, a lopi sweater. As soon as photos of the gifting were published in Iceland, people immediately freaked out over how badly made the sweater was, causing what *Iceland Magazine* called "significant outrage and criticism" and what delighted American journalists nicknamed "sweatergate." Particularly offensive was the odd neckline, which was so wide that Emanuel probably could have worn it as a skirt.[5] Hot on the trail of the truth, investigative reporters from Icelandic news conglomerate Visir identified the sweater as having been made in China and sold by 66° North, prompting a rebuke by the Handknitting Association of Iceland. A completely unscientific poll of Icelanders overwhelmingly said that the mayor should throw the sweater out rather than keep it.[6]

---

1. If you want to be pedantic, you already know that *lopi* actually means "roving band" in Icelandic—but pointing that out won't make you any friends at parties. For all practical purposes, *lopi* is used to refer specifically to Icelandic wool.
2. Guðrun Helgadóttir, "Nation in a Sheep's Coat: The Icelandic Sweater," *FORMakademisk* 4, no. 2 (2009).
3. Anna Kristine Magnúsdóttir, "Hún innleiddi lopapeysumynstur á Íslandi!" *Vikan* 7 (1998), 6–8; quoted in "Wool Is Gold" ("Ull er Gull"), by ethnologist Soffía Valdimarsdóttir.
4. See https://apnews.com/article/china-international-news-europe-iceland-624f27544cb44b489f46081738d9443d.
5. https://icelandmag.is/article/chicago-wool-jumper-scandal-ministry-spokesman-confirms-identity-jumper.
6. https://www.visir.is/g/2016160318664/lopapeysan-framleidd-i-kina.

Guitarist/singer Aðalbjörn Tryggvason from the Icelandic heavy metal band Sólstafir, with a lopapeysa he picked up at a thrift store and wears on stage around the world.

Knitting a Lopi in Iceland

I photographed one of Joan's knitting books in 2015 and was eager to photograph this one, but COVID had other plans, and both Iceland and the United States were shut down completely as our trip was set to begin in 2020. "How about this?" Joan suggested over the phone one evening in August. "Why don't I teach you how to knit over Zoom, and when we finally get to Iceland, you'll be able to knit a lopapeysa while we're there?" This sounded like a great idea. Knowing how to knit, I figured, would make me a better photographer of knitwear, and, in lockdown, I suddenly had a lot of time on my hands. We started with weekly lessons—learning how to hold the needles, how to make the stitches, and then how to diagnose the many, many terrible things I'd done wrong. My first thing, a sort of cowl, looked like the flag from a pirate ship after an epic battle, filled with holes, no two rows the same length . . . but as the weeks wore on, there came scarves and hats and gloves, and one by one I learned each of the elements required to make a lopi: knits, purls, increases, decreases, color work, and double-pointed needles. And slowly, it all started to make sense. My stitches got neater and more precise, and what had seemed impossible in August 2020 started to seem very likely by July 2021, when we packed our bags to finally begin our long-delayed trip to find out about this iconic piece of clothing.

Starting from scratch: learning to knit over Zoom so that I could make a lopi whenever we got to Iceland. Note Viking beard.

Getting Started

We set out for our Icelandic tour with five people—some knitters and some adventurers—and a desire to learn more about the place and its traditions.

Your ticket says you're flying into Reykjavik, but you're not. You're actually flying into Keflavik, 32 miles (52 km) to the west. When you land in Keflavik, you can get to the capital city in a variety of ways, the easiest of which is taking one of the frequent airport shuttles, but you can also rent a car, van, or motor home, all right from the airport. However you do it, Iceland is ready for you.

Iceland is a small country, about the size of Kentucky, populated by about 343,000 people, fully one-third of whom live in Reykjavik. The rest are scattered about, mostly along the coasts. Fishing has long been an important part of Iceland's history, and a lot of small fishing towns dot the outer rim of the country. There are so few people in Iceland, and they share so much DNA, that if you're looking for one Icelander, pretty much all you have to do is ask another Icelander: if they're not friends or related, they know someone who is.

We started with Kristinn Snær Agnarsson, a.k.a. Kiddi, a professional drummer who once worked with a band that I shot an album cover for. "Find Kiddi," they said when I mentioned I was going to Iceland. "He knows everyone."

"Do you know any knitters?" I asked Kiddi in an email.

"Of course," he answered. "Everybody in Iceland knits. I will introduce you to some people."

One set of people I was particularly interested in meeting were Sólstafir, Iceland's most popular heavy metal band who've featured lopapeysa sweaters prominently in their videos and concerts for twenty years. What is it about this sweater that makes it something a rock band would wear on stage? How is this gap bridged, from grandmothers to musicians to . . . everyone? Repeated emails to Sólstafir's management company had yielded nothing. So I asked Kiddi, "What about Sólstafir?"

"Of course," he says. "I know those guys."

The BSÍ bus terminal is where most Reykjavik adventures begin. It's a ten minute walk to town.

How Is Iceland Even . . . ?

Iceland is unique among all places in the world. It is literally a land of ice and fire, with glaciers and 120 volcanoes, both active and inactive. It has some of the most geologically unique, epic, and beautiful natural features on earth. How does this place even exist? We wanted to have some idea before we went, so we asked Dr. Matt Kuchta from the University of Wisconsin–Stout's Department of Geology, and he drew us some maps.

Iceland sits at the intersection of two tectonic plates, one that holds North America and one that holds Europe. The earth's mantle—the molten rock that fills the earth—is oozing up between these two plates, pushing America to the west and Europe to the east. This creates the world's longest mountain range, the not-so-cleverly-named mid-ocean ridge. It would be spectacular to look at, but it's thousands of feet beneath the sea, except for Iceland, where volcanic activity has pushed a humongous mountain out of the water.

"If you see a rock in Iceland," Matt said, "it came from a volcano," either in the form of lava or ash. Basalt is the type of stone that makes up everything here, from the mountains to the driveway gravel to the black beach sand. Matt added that there are indeed *some* rocks that aren't volcanic, but you have to spend some time looking for them, they're not visible everywhere, and you should be pretty excited if you find one. In the north and places in the east, a process called tectonic uplift has pushed the ocean floor up to the surface, and that has exposed some sedimentary rock. But you should feel pretty

confident in picking up any stone, turning to the person next to you, and saying, with great authority, "This is basalt. It's from a volcano."

There are eruptions, on average, every three years, and they all behave differently. Some of them, like 2010's Eyjafjallajökull, spew billions of tons of ash into the air, and others, like 2021's Fagradalsfjall, quietly ooze lava. How a volcano erupts depends on how the lava and the gas and any water interact. Katla, for example, an enormous, active volcano that sits in the south near the town of Vik, exists under the Myrdalsjökull ice cap, and when it inevitably erupts (it's due for a big one at any time), the eruption will melt millions of gallons of ice and flood everything downhill in addition to all the ash and lava it will fling across the landscape.

So what do you do with billions of tons of molten rock piled under your house? If you guessed, "Produce energy," you'd be correct. Nearly all of Iceland's electricity comes from renewable sources: geothermal and hydroelectric. The abundance of easily accessible magma also provides Icelanders with limitless hot water, so you can take a shower that lasts the whole day and it will never get cold. This also means that nearly every pool in Iceland is around the temperature of bathwater, and every town has public hot tubs where people often spend time soaking and talking to their neighbors, which you would do every day, too, if you had that many giant hot tubs in your neighborhood, no matter how boring your neighbors might be.

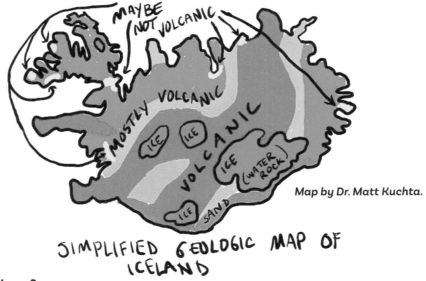

Map by Dr. Matt Kuchta.

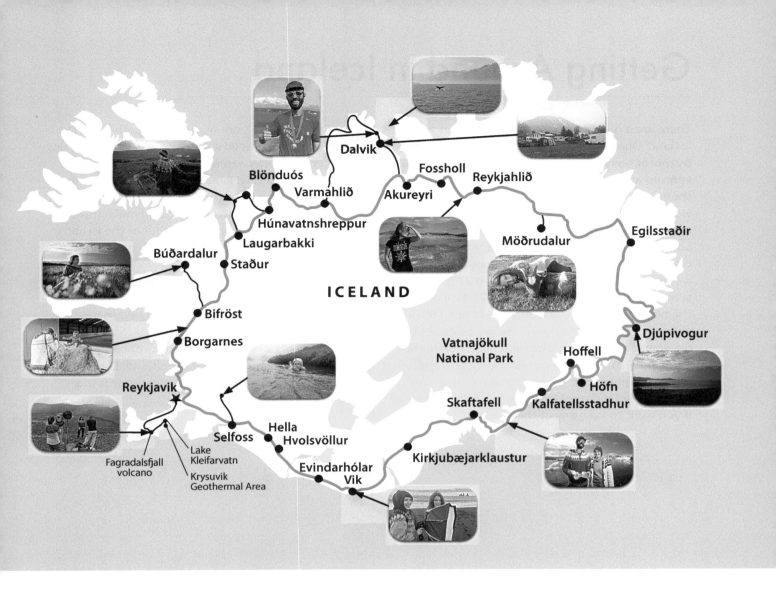

The Ring Road

You can certainly visit Iceland and have a wonderful time without ever venturing far from Reykjavik, but there are also some great ways to see more of the country. Route 1, a.k.a. Þjóðvegur 1, a.k.a. "the Ring Road," is a well-maintained, narrow, two-lane highway 821 miles (1,200 km) in length that mostly circumnavigates the island, leaving out the West Fjords, the North, and much of the East Fjords. This is a more adventurous trek for travelers.

It can be done in three days—it's the distance from Los Angeles to El Paso, so if you're used to driving across America, you may think, *Jeez, I can do that in a day*—but to see things and appreciate them, eight to ten days is much better.

If you have less time, there's also the "Golden Circle," which hits a lot of spectacular sites in just 500 miles (800 km), which is the distance from New York City to Charlotte, South Carolina.

Getting Around in Iceland

There are a number of popular ways to get around Iceland. One is by car, one is by van, and another is by motor home. Decide first how far you want to venture and how many comforts you want. Since there were five of us, we opted for the largest RV we could get.

Even with all that space, Alon and Arwin, our two adventurers, have brought along a tent and are planning on sleeping outside whenever they have a chance. They're going to give it a try right away since Alon wants to run a 15-mile (26-km) race in the north in two days and Joan and I need to do some interviews in Reykjavik. So our team splits up. Alon and Arwin get a car and head north; they'll come back in three days, grab the RV, and pick us up. In the meantime, we have much to do.

You'll need different vehicles for different things. If you want to take any of the "F roads" ("F" stands for *fjall*, meaning "mountain") that go through the highlands, you'll need a 4x4 because you'll be going over gravel, rocks, streams, and all sorts of stuff. The Ring Road is well maintained, but in the winter, unexpected snowstorms can make driving difficult, especially in the north, which could make traveling with an RV extra complicated. A lot of the F roads, because of the weather, aren't even open until June or July.

Check to make sure your insurance company covers international travel. If it doesn't, your credit card company might. If not, you'll need to get insurance when you rent your car.

Iceland honors American and European driver's licenses and also International Driving Permits, which you'll need if your license is in a nonroman alphabet.

Walking back from photographing at the beach in Vik. Everywhere you look in Iceland is breathtaking.

Inside the Hand Knitting Association.

Adventure: The Icelandic Hand Knitting Association

The shuttle from the airport leaves us at the BSI bus terminal in Reykjavik, just a few blocks from the center of town. We haul our relatively compact luggage through a beautiful neighborhood of one- and two-story houses, set far enough apart that everybody has a yard and nothing seems cramped. The point of reference to keep from getting lost is Hallgrímskirkja Church, with its gigantic spire rising far, far above the rest of the city. Though it seems older, Hallgrímskirkja was built starting in 1945 and not finished until the mid-1980s. When we get to the top of the hill, Joan pauses to point out designs in the paving stones. "I'm just going to take a photo of these," she says. "You never know when they'll be useful for a pattern." I look down at them, and say, "Hey, I could make my lopi out of these shapes, right?" Joan agrees. They'd make for an easy pattern for my first lopi.

"Let's stop at the Hand Knitting Association store and get you some wool then," Joan says.

Any knitting adventure in Iceland probably begins with a stop at the Hand Knitting Association, in Reykjavik. A knitter's paradise festooned with skeins of lopi wool, sweaters, and knitwear, it's a great place to stop for materials, equipment, inspiration, or gifts for the knitter in your life. And if you're not interested in wool, you can visit 12 Tónar records next door while your partner shops.

I pick out Léttlopi, which is vaguely two-stranded in very traditional colors. Joan thinks it a little ambitious, but I'm won over by the small stitches on some of the sweaters in the store and want to give it a try.

My yarn picked out and our bags stowed, it's time to see the town. We stop in at Bastard, one of the local bars just a few blocks from the Hand Knitting Association. It's a lively place filled with locals. Parliament is just a few blocks away, and the restaurant is popular with legislators and their staff. It's got a beautiful, curved wooden bar,

Hand Knitting Association: yarn in traditional and dyed colors.

Unspun wool at the Hand Knitting Association.

exposed brick walls, tall tables, and high, leather-covered benches.

Standing at the end of the bar next to a painting of a cat wearing a top hat made of flowers is a guy who looks like he must be an Icelandic movie star.

"Do you think he's an Icelandic movie star?" Trillian asks. We'd been binge-watching Icelandic movies for the last 14 months.

"He must be," I say. He's got a long beard, is wearing a black leather jacket, and is talking to a blond man with glasses who we imagine must be a famous Icelandic movie director.

When he moves closer to us to get the bartender's attention, I say, "Excuse me, are you an Icelandic movie star?" His eyes light up—he reaches one hand to grab his beard like he's wringing out a washcloth and answers in perfect English, "Why, yes, I am! Do I look like I am?" He smiles broadly, and I'm immediately glad I've spoken to him. It turns out his name is Mikael, and he's a computer programmer and occasional documentary TV host with a face like a Viking and a deep fondness for lopapeysas. "I have nine," he says, "they're just perfect for everything. They're like a part of you." Mikael recently starred in a series of Garmin watch ads that had him doing things like leaping over streams and sprinting through snow-covered rock fields. He looks very rugged. His friend Eyþór, a professor at Reykjavik Technical College, is head of the Icelandic robotics team and owner of an electric scooter company. I ask Eyþór if he has a lopapeysa. "No," he says, lifting a finger skyward, "and not that my grandmother doesn't keep begging to make me one. I just prefer modern fabrics; they're less bulky and they insulate better." Spoken like a scientist. I mention that we're writing a book about lopis and touring around the country looking for things to do. Mikael says he has nothing to do the next day and would be happy to take us around and show us some things. We stay for a while, but the jet lag starts to creep in, so we head off to our hotel. It's 10 o'clock at night, but it may as well be noon, because the sun is just hanging overhead like a chandelier. At the hotel, I close the blinds and fall asleep immediately.

Adventure: Helgufoss—A Waterfall, a Poet, and a Rock Filled (Possibly) with Trolls

The next morning, it's early, but we're eager to get started. It doesn't seem the sun has moved since we went to bed. We meet Mikael upstairs at Prikið, the oldest café in Reykjavik. We have food that may be breakfast or brunch or lunch or something only hobbits have a name for. It's summer so you can't tell what time it is. The sun doesn't really set between April and September. It hits the horizon at about 11:30 in the evening, rolls along for an hour or two, and then starts coming up again. By 3:30 in the morning, it's like living inside a light bulb.

Looking out the window into the street below, we see people ambling slowly by.

"Everybody in Iceland has three lopapeysa," Mikael explains, refilling his coffee cup from a pot the waiter has left for us, "one that their mother knitted them, one their grandmother knitted them, and one that someone left at their house after a party."

After we finish eating, someone says they want to see a waterfall, and Mikael suggests we go to Helgufoss. "It's a nice ride through the country," he says. "It's right behind the house of Halldór Laxness. There will be horses." Mikael is wearing a cardigan lopi knitted by his friend Yljia from a popular Icelandic pattern. A few months previous, I was horrified to learn from Joan that the way to make a cardigan is to just make a sweater and then cut it in half with a pair of scissors and sew buttons on it.

Halldór Kiljan Laxness was the first, and only, Icelander to win the Nobel Prize for Literature and as such was a gigantic personality in Iceland. Writer of novels, translator of Voltaire and Hemingway, Laxness was born in 1902. He lived to be 96 years old in a small but elegant country house swaddled within a magnificent landscape. Helgufoss is a waterfall about three miles (five km) from the house. To get there, start out in Laxness's driveway and hike along the stream until you come to a giant rock known as Helguholl. The Icelandic Sagas (specifically the 14th-century saga *Bárðar saga Snæfellsáss*) tell us that Helga was the daughter of a troll named Bárður Snæfellsás. They have a difficult relationship, and ultimately, she walks into

Figuring out what to do. Mikael in Prikið in a lopi knitted by Yljia Linnet.

the stone, where she remains to this day, possibly with elves.

"Is it true that before you can do roadwork an inspector needs to come and certify that no elves live there?" I ask Mikael, seeming to remember that I'd heard that on the radio at some time in the past.

"Well . . . yes," he says, "but elf inspector isn't a full-time job. It's just someone around the office who they can put on TV for a light news story. They just come out and say, 'We've inspected this area and it's clear of elves,' or 'We waited until the elves had moved to a new place before we continued construction,' and it's on the news and everybody has a pleasant feeling about road construction."

Laxness's house appears suddenly on the right. It's very unassuming and largely hidden behind small trees. ("What do you do if you're lost in an Icelandic forest?" goes a popular joke. "Stand up!" is the answer.) You can park in the driveway. There are spaces for about five cars. Walk out back from the house, and you'll see a beautiful swimming pool and a stream that it intersects with. The novelist used to walk back here for inspiration. In fact, the trail from the house to the falls is called the Poet's Path.

Mikael at Helguholl wearing a sweater knitted by his friend Yljia from a popular Icelandic pattern.

Trillian enjoying the view from the Poet's Path.

It's impossible to overestimate the importance of Laxness in Icelandic culture. His 1935 novel *Sjálfstætt Fólk* (translated as *Independent People*) is regarded as one of the greatest books of the 20th century, and not just in Iceland. Laxness's Nobel Prize for Literature is not the only reason this house is an important stop for us. There's the story that Auður Sveinsdóttir Laxness created the first lopapeysa. I'd love to know more details directly, but Auður died on Halloween 2012 at the age of 94, so we can't ask her.[1] What we do know after talking to people at the Hand Knitting Association is that she was a knitting instructor, editor of several knitting magazines, and she started making sweaters with colorful yokes sometime in the late 1940s. So while she might not have been the first, she was certainly in the right place to have been

Auður Sveinsdóttir Laxness in an early lopi, probably 1950s. Photo courtesy of Gljúfrasteinn, the Laxness museum in Mosfellsdalur.

1. https://grapevine.is/mag/articles/2014/05/05/screaming-jumpers.

one of the first, to have helped it become popular, and to have influenced its design.

The hike from Laxness's house is over very rough terrain; stout hiking boots will keep your feet from feeling pummeled at the end. There are no paths or signs to guide you. At times the passage is treacherous, and a misstep may send you sliding to the stream below, so watch your footing. Likewise, there are no water fountains or bathrooms or souvenir shops and, in fact, likely no other people.

As far as waterfalls go, Gullfoss is larger, but you have to buy tickets first and then share the view

At the top of Helgufoss.

with hundreds of tourists all angling for the same Instagram photo. At Helgufoss, you can climb to the top and shout your barbaric *Yawp* without a soul hearing you, except maybe some elves.

We leave our things at the bottom of the falls and hike to the summit, where the marvelous stream bubbles briskly across stones before plummeting 40 feet. We stand there for a while and then climb down and hike back through the fields of lupins blooming bright and purple. Then back to Reykjavik we go, to settle in before getting started on our tour.

Adventure: The Hot Springs at Skátalaug

The next morning, Kiddi and his girlfriend, Guðný, show up while we're at the café. Prikið has kind of become our base station. There's a huge upstairs and friendly staff and good food that can be eaten leisurely. Kiddi suggests that we visit a hot spring. He's also contacted Sólstafir and informs us that their guitar player, Sæþór, would be happy to talk to us about sweaters.

"His wife, Rä, is American," Kiddi adds. "You should meet her too."

Joan and I working at Prikið. If you're going to journal your trip, you need to do it every day or you'll forget everything. Photo by Trillian Stars.

Kiddi's wearing an extremely intricate brown lopi from a pattern called Riddari, by Védís Jónsdóttir, Iceland's most famous lopi designer. It's one of the most popular lopi patterns in the world and looks like an explosion of virtuoso knitting. Guðný has a beautiful gray lopi with fading grays and almost-purple blacks. It turns out Kiddi's mother made both of them. "She made me this one that I'm wearing...maybe eight years ago?...and I've worn it a lot, and she insisted on making me a new one for Christmas, which is this gray one, but it was a little snug. I think in her mind I'm still 12, so it's Guðný's now," he says, with a laugh, adding, "I didn't give it to her; she just decided to take it."

But one thing that we're learning is that there's magic in a sweater that's borrowed, lent, or bestowed. And there will be more.

"My mother knits," says Kiddi, "watching some docudrama or crime show on TV, and it's like she's on autopilot."

"I think it's just such a big part of our culture," says Guðný, "and it's a big part of our childhoods. And it's also very practical. I own four sweaters—"

"Apart from this one she stole from me," interjects Kiddi.

"Yes," she agrees, "four others, and I wear them all year round. When I was little, it was always an important part of the autumn to go visit my great-grandmother and to pick out new socks for the winter. Knitting's always been there, and we always use these things; it's always nice to have them."

I feel the power of this gift. Guðný's memory suddenly makes me nostalgic for my own long-gone grandmother as in a flash, I recall the memory of going to her house to spend the weekend and her asking me to pick out colors for an afghan she was going to crochet for me. I picked red, white, and blue because it was 1976, and that weekend, while we watched TV and talked and ate and played, the blanket got bigger and bigger, and I carried it with me when I left Sunday night. And I still have it; it's on my bed.

Kiddi also becomes nostalgic about the sweater he's wearing right now. "I love this sweater!" he says enthusiastically, as if he's just discovered it for the first time. "It's so comfortable! I don't know if I've slept in it...actually, I'm pretty sure I have. This one has been all over the world touring."

"What's the farthest it's been from home?" Joan asks.

"It's been to Australia," Kiddi says, thinking, "though I didn't need it in Australia in January, so I don't think I wore it there, but I left from New York, where it was really cold. But, let's get going! We have some things to show you!"

The earth beneath Iceland is bubbling lava—the entire island is a cone filled with molten magma. In some places, the geothermal activity is closer to the surface than in other places. One of these is Seltún, which is about 25 miles (40 km) south of Reykjavik. There you can see solfataras, literally

Guðný and Kiddi in front of racks of drying codfish heads. The heads are mostly exported and used in soups. The rest of the fish, known as harðfiskur, are eaten by Icelanders from bags, like potato chips or jerky, and have been an Icelandic tradition for centuries. The Reykjavik Grapevine, the local newspaper mostly for tourists, calls harðfiskur "the candy of the north." Kiddi's and Guðný's sweaters were both made by Kiddi's mother.

"sulphur places," deposits of sulfur and other minerals that begin to form themselves into shapes like mounds and tubes; and fumaroles, cracks in the earth's surface that release volcanic gases and steam. These areas of geothermal activity are not only really beautiful and strange looking, but they have unexpected practical benefits in the form of hot springs—places where boiling water bubbles up to the surface and then cools, forming bathwater-temperature ponds.

The Blue Lagoon is the most famous of these. Just a few minutes from the Keflavik airport, it's Iceland's number-one tourist attraction: a beautiful, blue, enormous, warm, delightful lake with swim-up bars, wooden walkways, indoor changing areas, and carefully managed views. While its irregular shape may make it look like a natural wonder, the Blue Lagoon is actually the tailings pond for the Svartsengi geothermal power plant. In 1976, engineers for HS Orka dug a hole 1.2 miles (2 km) down into the rock and released high-pressure

steam at a blistering 570 degrees Fahrenheit (299 C). The steam blasts up through pipes with a powerful ferocity and turns a turbine, which generates electricity. As the steam cools into water after its incredible journey from (not quite) the center of the earth, it's piped into 21,000 homes for shower water and also into the Blue Lagoon, where tourists splash around in it. The lagoon is so popular that you need reservations days in advance.

Kiddi suggests that we meet up with Rä and Sæþór and visit a hot spring in the middle of nowhere, called Skátalaug. He makes a call, and we pack up our things and head downstairs. A few minutes later, Rä and Sæþór pull up and get out of the car, looking like a pair of rock stars in lopi sweaters and motorcycle boots. We say hello and introduce ourselves. Rä does most of the talking while Sæþór stares off into the distance, like an album cover. I'm a little nervous because I've been watching Sólstafir concerts on YouTube relentlessly for the past 14 months. Trillian and I pile in the car with them, and Joan rides with Kiddi and Guðný.

"The Blue Lagoon is nice," Rä says as we drive through remote snow-dusted hills, "but who wants to deal with all those people?" Iceland is a country of only a few people. And Reykjavik, while it's the largest city, is a bit like an American shore town. There are no skyscrapers, no crowded streets, no hustle, no bustle. Icelanders appreciate a little bit of space and quiet.

Powered by the geothermal area known as Seltún, it's actually difficult to find Skátalaug even when you know exactly where it is (and here's exactly where it is: 63°54'14. 22°02'35.9" W). A little off-roading is necessary, but if you're careful, your car can make it. Or you can park by the road and walk about 500 feet (150 m). Look for the bright-green vegetation, which grows around the springs, and follow it up to the top of a flat hill. Once there, you'll find a pond about 10 feet (3 m) across and 20 feet (6 m) long. There's no changing station (in fact, there's nothing at all), so put your swimsuit on in the glory of nature realizing there's probably not another person for five miles (8 km) in any direction, or change in your car.

It feels weird to stand at the side of a pond in 40 degree F (4 C) weather—your senses tell you it's going to be freezing, but it's like bathwater, and soaking in a hot spring in the cold weather is something of an Icelandic national pastime.

From the hot springs at Skátalaug, you can look down onto Kleifarvatn lake, and when you've parboiled yourself long enough, you can relax in the brisk air by the side of the spring and read *The Draining Lake*, a detective novel about Kleifarvatn by Icelandic crime novelist Arnaldur Indriðason, in which receding lake water reveals the body of a long-hidden murder victim. The book is spooky and wonderfully written, making it obvious why Indriðason is one of Iceland's most famous writers. If you're a diver, there are spectacular underwater hot springs in the lake itself, pumping blistering water up into the basin slightly slower than it's draining out into some subterranean reservoir.

We spend a lovely half hour marveling that such a thing can be possible—that out here in the nowhere is a private slice of paradise. You regulate your temperature by rising a bit out of the water until you think ice may form on you and then lowering yourself back in. When nobody can take any more tranquility and relaxation, we decide to visit nearby Seltún.

Trillian and Joan in the hot spring.

Sæþór and Rä in their traditional lopis. For natives and immigrants alike, having a lopi gives you a sense of belonging.

"My in-laws gave me my lopapeysa for Yule the first year that I was here," Rä says. "It was their way of welcoming me into the family and saying I was one of them. It made me feel like I belonged."

"I have ... two," says Sæþór, thinking carefully. "They were both gifts. I got one at a farm, the other one ... I want to say it was my grandmother who gave it to me, but not really, it was an old person, a family friend like a grandmother, who knitted it by herself." Knitwear is a common gift in Iceland. Sæþór remembers getting ... "*Vettlingar?*" he asks Rä, pointing at his hand, "one here and one here?" "Mittens," she tells him. "Ah yes, mittens. You would always get mittens as a child." Like many people in Iceland, Sæþór learned to knit when he was nine, but he doesn't do it anymore. Receiving knitwear as gifts is baked into Icelandic tradition. In America, children may sigh at the thought of another Christmas of socks and underwear, but in Iceland, children tear through packages hoping to find wool because Jólakötturinn, the gigantic, fearsome, monster cat of Grýla the witch, wanders the countryside on Christmas eating children who

Behind the scenes. Kiddi tries out photographing with my light setup while I play the part of the Voice-Activated Light Stand. At Seltún.

Sæþór wearing his lopi in the video for "Fjara," from the album Svartir Sandar. *The video features the landscape around the southern town of Vík í Mýrdal and was directed by Bowen Staines.*

didn't get clothes as presents. In fact, the whole of Icelandic Christmas mythology is a terrifying literature aimed at keeping children on their best behavior. Grýla and her hideous, malevolent children, the Yule Lads, spend weeks banging around the countryside, performing horrific acts, putting bad children in sacks and carting them off to evil fates.

I ask Sæþór about wearing his lopapeysa onstage and in music videos, like the video for "Fjara," where a woman drags a coffin across the epic landscape around Vík í Mýrdal—including past the wreckage of a US Navy DC-3 that crashed there in 1973. He doesn't spend much time thinking about it. He shrugs: "It was just my thought to use it." He says he imagined that in this video, he was the ghost of a kindly farmer, and it seemed appropriate. Now we're learning that, in Iceland, farmers and rock stars must have considerable overlap in their closets.

Down comes Grýla
from the hills
With forked tails,
Sword in hand,
Coming to cut out the
stomachs of the children
Who cry for meat in Lent.

"Grýla," from *Icelandic Folktales and Legends*, by Jón Árnason

Adventure: Heavy Metal Horses

Kiddi's not done pulling rabbits out of hats. He calls the next morning to say that we can meet Aðalbjörn Tryggvason, or Addi as he's called, the frontman for Sólstafir, at their rehearsal space overlooking the ocean on the west coast. When we get there, we find the space is packed with custom guitars made by master Icelandic luthier Gunnar Örn Sigurdsson, who carves them and then dips them in boiling, sulfurous hot-spring water to temper and color them. For two and a half decades, Sólstafir has roared through festivals around the world bringing their thundering, melodic, and very Icelandic sound to fans everywhere, with the inevitability of a glacier moving to the sea. Equal parts Pink Floyd and Black Sabbath, their music is formed by the crucible of Iceland's landscape where fire and ice meet. And completely unlike all American heavy metal bands, hand-knitted sweaters feature prominently in their videos and everyday stage wear. In fact, Addi's wearing one right now. "I got this for thirty dollars, used," he tells us, tugging at his sleeve to examine a large hole forming around the elbow. "I'd had one very much

like it that belonged to my grandmother. It was blue; I wore it forever on tour and lost it somewhere and just missed it. So when I saw this one, I just bought it. I didn't really think anything about it; it's not 'cool'—it's not fashion—it's just something that you'd wear every day to keep warm. It's survived a few tours, but when you're onstage and you play guitar, it starts to fall apart at the right wrist and the left elbow first, so it needs to be patched."

When we press about the significance of the lopi, Addi shrugs.

"Don't overthink it," he says. "It's just a sweater. I just come from that generation, everybody's grandmom was making them. They're everywhere."

But surely there's something about the tradition? A sweater that your grandmom made can't be the same as the ones that tourists are buying. Addi agrees that this is true.

"I had another one once," he recalls, "that someone gave me for Christmas; it was a trendier one, very hipster, but it wasn't made the same as this one. It wasn't as thick, and once it started falling apart at the right wrist, it was as though it

Addi in Sólstafir's rehearsal space; lopi from a thrift store.

had leprosy. It just vaporized. This one, if I fix the elbows and the wrists, I'm pretty sure it will outlive me, but the hipster one was done.

"I remember being ten," Addi continues, "and they were teaching me to knit, and it was the most boring stuff. 'Why would I do this?' I thought, 'I have a grandmother.'" But he has kept up with sewing, which is useful on the road when things come apart. "When your pants rip on stage, that's not too good," he says. "You should probably fix that."

Joan notices a strange piece of metal connecting his guitar to the strap and recognizes that it's a horse bit.

"What's the story of that?" she wants to know.

"Ah! That's a horse bit. Do you like horses? I have horses."

Joan likes horses. She also has a horse. So we pile into Addi's Jeep and head out to his horse farm.

Like the sheep, horses came to Iceland with the Vikings a thousand years ago and have remained—also like the sheep—without intermixing with any other types of horse, making them the most purebred horses in the world, which is something Icelanders are interested in keeping up. They're so concerned about it that if you take an Icelandic horse out of Iceland, it can never come back. One of the benefits of this is that there are very few equine diseases on the island, though farmers prefer that you don't pet the horses you may see on the side of the road, because diseases that do exist can be passed from horse to hand to horse.

The most instantly recognizable thing about them is that Icelandic horses are significantly smaller in stature than other horses.

"Don't call them ponies," Addi says as we get out of the Jeep. "It makes them self-conscious."

We walk up a short road with a view out over dark green fields that stretch to the horizon. There's a fenced-in space for horses to run and a low, one-story building.

"Oh, hello, you!" says Joan to each horse when we go in, and she hugs each one. And they're very excited to see people. In fact, one of them gets extremely jealous if other horses are getting attention and he isn't, so Joan spends most of her time with her arms wrapped around his neck like they're dancing at the prom. And the horse is quiet, and Joan is quiet, and it's like they're the only two people on earth. I ask Addi if I can photograph him with one of his horses outside. He says yes. The life of a rock star is, after all, comprised largely of being photographed.

We head back to Reykjavik.

Addi with his horse; lopi from a thrift store.

Rebekka at the lake.

Knitter Profile:
Rebekka Guðleifsdóttir

When you ask about new lopapeysa designers, one name comes up over and over and over again. It would be impossible to talk about the modern evolution of the lopi sweater without talking about Rebekka Guðleifsdóttir, whose stunning designs use color and shading to create gentle gradients. Her very new takes are still very identifiable as lopis and pay homage to the original.[1]

It seems there's nothing that this artist from Hafnarfjörður, Iceland, doesn't do well. She first broke onto the international stage in 2005, when she became the most popular photographer on the photo-sharing website Flickr. Her stunning, clever, and creative self-portraits eventually landed her a deal with Toyota and a book deal with Ilex Press. The *Wall Street Journal* dubbed her "The Web's Top

Photographer." Lately she's been flying drones and capturing Iceland from above, but throughout it all, she's been knitting.

"Let's go for a ride," she says in flawless English, and starts to tell us about her love affair with knitting.

"I usually choose the colors first, and after some necessary calculations to figure out how many stitches a new pattern should be, I literally just take a pencil and a notebook of graph paper and start making dots, it's very much just off the top of my head in an organic way."

She started out her art career making hyperrealistic pencil drawings at the age of 13, an obsession she had planned to continue exploring once she was accepted into Iceland's Academy

1. You can find some of her work at https://www.ravelry.com/patterns/sources/rebekkagudleifs-designs.

of the Arts, from which she earned her BA in visual arts.

"I didn't agree with my professors about much while I was in art school, but what irked me the most was their obvious disdain for drawing from photos. They claimed it wasn't art but craftsmanship. In a way I'm glad they tried to get me to do other things (I never actually stopped drawing), because ultimately that led me to exploring digital photography and Photoshop—another thing my professors weren't fond of. I'd already learned darkroom work and film stuff a few years earlier, but Photoshop allowed me to create with my camera the scenes that I had always envisioned I would perhaps paint. I had always imagined I'd advance from drawing and learn to paint in art school. That never happened."

It was during her time in art school that her passion for knitting was truly ignited.

"A guy I was dating back then had a wool sweater with a hood that his mom had made. I thought it was kind of cool, and he asked if I wanted her to make me one, which I briefly considered but then decided that since I'd never actually met the woman, I'd rather just try and do it myself."

Her own mother is an excellent knitter but back then had never designed things, always sticking to patterns in magazines. "Mom helped me get started on a sweater from a seventies magazine. I hadn't knit anything since in my teens, and it took me months to finish. I posted a picture of myself wearing it on Flickr and got a lot of feedback. I started a second one right away, where I altered the pattern a little bit and made it much more formfitting than any wool sweater I'd ever seen. I was completely hooked by then and decided to make a third, where I'd design the pattern from scratch. It's like something had been missing from my life. I enjoyed the process so much. After posting a picture of this third sweater, mentioning that it was my own design, I got my first request for a custom-made sweater, from a woman in the US. That's what really kicked things off, and with each new sweater I made and posted on Flickr, more requests came pouring in, from all over the world. I had a waiting list twenty deep. At some point I decided that I'd set myself a limit for these one-of-a-kind, custom-made sweaters, stopping after a hundred."

She worked like this for almost a decade, during which time she realized she'd become somewhat famous as the modern face of the Icelandic sweater.

"There was a time," she says, "where if you just googled 'lopapeysa,' you just saw my sweaters." And even now with the internet diluted by billions of images, Rebekka's sweaters fill page after page after page on sites like Pinterest.

After reaching her goal of 100 sweaters, Rebekka felt a bit lost.

"It was a really great art project but a horrible business model. Because now I'd spent countless hours creating all these amazing sweaters but wasn't technically allowed to reuse the patterns. And I hadn't really charged nearly enough for that to have been worthwhile.

"Luckily for me, a German knitter, Christine Knoller, had been following my progress for years. She reached out in 2018 and offered me a partnership. I would create new sweater prototypes, and she would do the boring technical work of turning them into patterns that could be sold. This was something I'd been thinking of doing and had even tried making a PDF pattern myself, but I hated how complicated it was to translate my vision into something a person could actually follow and replicate. Thanks to Christine, I now have five patterns up on Ravelry, and she does a ton of promoting to her many followers in Germany. It's been a great partnership, which I look forward to continuing."

Lopapeysa by Rebekka. Photo by Rebekka Guðleifsdóttir.

"For me," she says, "my approach to the lopapeysa was definitely taking something old and making something new from it. And when people told me you can't do that, it really made me want to do it more—challenge accepted. It was fun to take this kind of farmer look and make it into something a little bit more sexy and contemporary."

Some of the things she likes are zipped hoodies, high collars, tailored waists, and thumbholes, but she's still not sure if she's the one who made them popular. "Maybe I did," she says, when pressed. "I don't know. I've heard people say that. But who knows." Popular photography blogger David Hobby, a.k.a. "The Strobist," warns in his April 2007 blog post about Rebekka that she is "prone to attacks of modesty."

Whether she was maybe the driving force in the evolution of the lopi or, like Auður Laxness, one of a myriad of design influences, Rebekka is both visionary and driven. "I feel incomplete every time I finish a project and I don't have another one," she says. The urge to keep creating is unquenchable. She takes her knitting to the movies, and she's taken it to the orchestra, where she has sat in the front row stitching away. She's part of a group of people trying to hang on to a part of history and keep it relevant.

"Young people trying to make new sweaters isn't really a thing in Iceland. They're not really wearing

Halldór drove for an hour to fish, wearing a sweater his grandmother knitted for his brother two decades ago.

them either, except on camping trips, where people sit around drinking and get chilly. Many women my age do knit but almost exclusively from patterns. I feel that it's kind of dying out, like home cooking and doing things not related to your smartphone. It's still common that retired grandmothers are making the sweaters you find in the stores, and sadly, they're getting paid almost nothing for it."

If you get a tourist sweater, she tells us, it's likely either machine-made in China or it's hand-knit in Iceland by underpaid senior citizens, something that sets her teeth on edge. "Some of these women are getting paid in nothing more than wool. Lopis are expensive; they take a lot of time."

While we talk, Rebekka's taking us to Kleifarvatn, which we'd seen yesterday in the distance from the hot spring.

"It's one of my secret spots," she says.

Rebekka at Lake Kleifarvatn.

We pull off the road and walk out along a hidden spit of land along the lake.

"I did a self-portrait here years ago," she says. "I borrowed this giant antique boat anchor from someone. It was like a hundred pounds [45 kg], and I lugged it through the tall grass over to the edge of this cliff here, where I posed with it. I was too tired to get it back in the car, so I left it here, meaning to come back and fetch it later. It was out of sight from the road, so I felt that wasn't too much of a risk. I may have sort of forgotten about it for almost a year, and when I did come back to get it, it was gone. I was extremely baffled. Who takes an iron boat anchor?"

Kleifarvatn lake is at the exact meeting of the east and west Mid-Atlantic tectonic plates. It has no tributaries; all its water comes in from fissures in the ground. In 2000, there was an earthquake that split the bottom, and it's been slowly draining, since more water leaves than comes in.

We take some photos, and a fisherman passes us, wearing a very nice lopi. "Can you tell me about your lopapeysa?" I burst out as he passes. His name is Halldór. He's wearing chest waders, and he's perfectly happy, if not baffled, to talk about his sweater.

"My grandmother knitted it," he says, "twenty years ago—for my brother." He shrugs, "It's mine now." He taps it and looks down at it as if he forgot that he was wearing it. I feel as though I may as well have inquired about a drawer full of socket wrenches. I ask if he thinks about his grandmother every time he wears this sweater. "Well," he admits, "no. But I am now because you asked me." He laughs and asks how much longer I want to talk about sweaters. He's more interested in fish.

Iceland holds on tight to its handcrafted traditions. Knitting is a required class in school. And there is an intersection of function and fashion that I haven't really figured out yet.

Knitter Profile: Pálína Gunnarsdóttir

It's still early after the lake visit, so we meet up again with Eyþór downtown. He's working with his robotics team at Reykjavik Technical. In a large classroom with all the desks and chairs pushed to the side, students—with not a lopapeysa in sight—are assembling wheels and motors, and swiftly they've come up with a first design based on no plans but just their best guesses as to how it should perform. They set the robot, which looks like a low, square tangle of coat hangers, on the floor, and it zooms around performing tasks while they discuss ways to improve it. One of the students lets Trillian drive, and it becomes immediately obvious how skilled you need to be to control it properly.

Eyþór's team beat the United States at the 2018 world championships in Mexico City. When the team looked at the task list, they realized their robot was hopelessly outpowered by the gargantuan American entry—which was incredibly well suited for performing impressive feats of strength. Then one of the team members realized they could use their robot's speed and small size to avoid the American behemoth entirely, perform a number of lower-point tasks repetitively and quickly, and—doing fast math in their heads—win.

"I've never felt a stronger surge of raw nationalism go through my body," says Eyþór, like Clark Kent taking off his glasses, "than when our ragtag alliance of Iceland, the Maldives, and Colombia beat the US in a sudden-death bracket. At the time we thought it was biblical—like David versus Goliath or something. The US may be a global superpower who split the atom, but we beat them at robotics."

As the coach, Eyþór stood on the sidelines, watching and pacing, while the team contemplated and developed their strategy.

"I understood for the first time," he says, "why people watch sports."

The team's tasks completed for the day, they pack up and start to drift out of the room, leaving the four of us.

"Do you want to go for a drive and meet my frænka Palla?" Eyþór asks, "She was born in 1930 and has been knitting for more than seventy-five years. She'd love to talk about it with you. I'll have to go as well, because she doesn't speak a word of English." We eagerly agree and pile into a little blue car for a day trip north.

I ask about this word, *frænka*. Eyþór tells us that Icelanders don't have specific words for "aunt" and

The national robotics team building next year's robot.

"uncle." Instead they have generic words: *frænka* meaning "female relative" and *frændi* meaning "male relative." Sometimes Icelanders we meet, like Sæþór two days before, struggle to figure out exactly how they're related to someone they're introducing us to. "My personal theory, not supported by any linguist," says Eyþór, "is that this is because family relations used to be so much more complex in Iceland. We don't intermarry so much anymore," he laughs, "but I'm not really the best person to ask about it, because I can't really be bothered. Would you like to listen to some Icelandic music? Tell me what music you like, and I'll find the Icelandic equivalent and I'll probably sing along."

The little blue car makes its way north from Reykjavik through fields of lupins as we call out the names of musicians we're familiar with. "Frank Sinatra!" we shout. "In Iceland that would be Raggi Bjarna!" says Eyþór, waving a finger in the air and then directing his phone to play Raggi Bjarna. "The Beatles!" we shout next. Eyþór's eyes light up. "Ah! That would be Hljómar!" And true to his word, he sings along in Icelandic as we drive through a tunnel beneath a fjord, listening to music.

This endeavor occupies the better part of an hour through mountains, over streams, and past fields of flowers. A lot of Hljómar's songs are just European songs with Icelandic lyrics, which is baffling to us. "This is about a sad, rural farmer," says Eyþór, singing Icelandic words to the tune of "California Dreaming."

> *Næðir dimm um grund*
> *norðanhríðin köld*
> *Nauðar rjáfrum í seint um vetrarkvöld*
> *Í svartamyrkri gljúpu*
> *svefninn linar þraut*
> *Sveitapiltsins draumur ber*
> *hann þá á braut.*[1]

"This was very popular to do in the nineteen sixties and seventies," says Kiddi later, when we ask about it. "It's like half a cover, because they'd just write Icelandic lyrics to an existing song. It was a crazy awakening for some Icelandic musicians in the nineteen nineties, when European music companies came along and said, 'You can't publish this song, it's not your song,' and the whole country came to a reckoning with international copyright law almost overnight."

Raggi Bjarna (a.k.a. Ragnar Bjarnason) does sound quite a bit like Frank Sinatra. He was born in 1934, started recording in the mid-1950s, and had a storied career that lasted until his death in February 2020. His popularity soared in the '70s, when he began doing duets with a younger popular singer, Ellý Vilhjálms, whose troubled life and premature death were the subject of a 2019 musical called *Ellý*, which played at the Reykjavik opera house for an unheard-of 200 nights to sold-out audiences. Every night, Raggi showed up after the show to play onstage with the cast and orchestra. What a strange experience that must have been.

(When we mention this to Kiddi later, he says, "Ah, yes! Raggi Bjarna! I have played with him quite a number of times.")

"How do you even pronounce this?" I ask, looking at the map and trying to figure out where we're going. "Hvammsfjörður? I don't even know what some of these letters are."

"Well," says Eyþór, "there are two letters that you'll see a lot that you don't have in English. There's ð," he says, drawing it in the air with his finger, "the letter *eth*, which is pronounced *th* like in the word *this*, and there's *thorn*, Þ, which is also pronounced *th* like in *thing*. This letter used to be in the English alphabet, but they stopped using it about the time they invented movable type, and instead they'd use the letter *y* since they weren't often used together and they had extras. So if you see a sign that says "Ye Old Store," it really just means 'The Old Store.'"

"How do you know this?" I ask. "Why didn't I learn this from a native English speaker?"

"Oh," says Eyþór, "I really don't know anything about orthography. I just read the Wikipedia page about *thorn* because it's in my name."

Another band Eyþór plays, after I request the Icelandic equivalent of Black Sabbath, is HAM, a heavy metal outfit and the house band in the cult classic film *Sodoma Reykjavik*, which we'd just watched a couple of weeks ago. The guitar player, Óttarr Proppé, became Iceland's minister of health in 2017, and his band opened for industrial metal juggernauts Rammstein on two tours in Iceland.

---

1. "The cold, dark storm blows over the ground./The rafters howl late in the winter evening./In the darkness, sleep eases the pain./ The farm boy's dream then carries him away."

We're still listening to HAM, and while I'm trying to picture them giving health advice, Eyþór points at a farm approaching on the right.

"Want to stop for ice cream?" he asks. "I used to go to this place all the time, but I probably haven't been since I was twelve." We pull into the dirt parking lot. Fields of meandering cows surround it, and some pigs roll lazily in the grass, snorting with excitement as we walk past. Inside an open barn is a shop selling lopi sweaters (of course) as well as various milk products (there were also vegan sorbets) and ice cream available in cups or cones. (There are also a variety of milk products I've never seen before, each labeled with the name of the cow that produced them and a freezer full of steaks, not labeled with the name of the cow that produced them.) Eating our ice cream in the fresh air outside, we walk through a small mix of amusements—swings, bouncy castles, trampolines—and sit in the sun. Children run past us squealing; an Icelandic sheep dog with a curled tail runs excitedly around in a circle trying to herd them before finally settling under our picnic table. We relax and enjoy the view and the break before getting back in the car and driving north through fields of lupins along the Snæfellsnes peninsula.

Eyþór's frænka, Palla, lives in a retirement home in the small (population about 275) village of Búðardalur, about two hours north of Reykjavik. For the past 91 years, she's lived a life continually infused with and surrounded by knitting. She's very happy to see us. Her apartment has a large sliding door that opens to a view of the sea, and she's surrounded by yarn, needles, tapestries, paintings, and photographs.

"Come in! Come in!" she says in Icelandic.

We sit down, and Palla begins to produce knitwear from every drawer in her apartment as well as photo albums and collections of patterns and hand-drawn notions of all sorts. It's just a gold mine of fiber arts history. We sit in rapt attention as she talks.

When she was 14, Palla's grandmother taught her to knit in the coastal village of Brelðutdrfa, where she lived in a turf house with her family. That year, a shipwreck stranded a group of sailors from the Faroe Islands; they washed up on the shore, and the townspeople looked for places to house them while they awaited rescue. A neighbor who put some of them up became fascinated with the unique three-dimensional stitch pattern on some of the sailors' sweaters. She taught herself how to make the design and showed it to Palla, who has made it part of her signature style for the past 77 years. She calls it "Faroese," and she's used it on sweaters, blankets, hats, and scarves ever since; it's become part of everything she does.

Palla indeed does not speak a word of English, so our conversations pass through Eyþór, who listens carefully, nods, asks an occasional question, and then turns and regurgitates what he's taken in, in two languages and both directions.

"Years later," he says, getting back to the story, "there was another shipwreck off the coast. This one was very bad, and six of the sailors had to be decapitated by the villagers." We recoil in horror, and Eyþór senses something from our

Palla and Eyþór discuss the knitting style from the Faroese sailors that she learned as a child and still incorporates into her work.

"You have a great understanding of the spirit of the lopi"— the O.G. seal of approval—as Palla admires one of Joan's lopi sweaters (making a good day great).

Palla's brothers wearing early versions of what would eventually evolve into the lopi sweater.

dumbstruck faces. "Wait," he says, "that's maybe not the right word. Dismembered. They had to be dismembered!" We still look horrified, frozen still with eyes like puffin eggs, visions of Palla producing an axe from a drawer flashing through our minds. Eyþór squints. "What is the word where you have an injured limb removed by a doctor?"

"Amputated?" offers Joan after a long pause.

"Ah, yes! Six sailors had to have amputations. I am sorry!"

We all exhale.

Palla and the rest of the townspeople thought it was miraculous, but every one of the injured seamen survived. Those sailors, though, brought with them no knitting revelations.

Since those days, Palla's made lopapeysa sweaters for everyone in her family. "We didn't really have patterns in the early days," she says. "You'd see a sweater, and you'd just look at it and know how it was made"—all the elements were part of a common though evolving vocabulary of stitches and color.

In the past 30 years or so, she's frequently drifted from the very traditional styles to add Icelandic horses (which she loves), sheep, and even helicopters, which adorn the yokes of lopis she created for two young frændi. Her designs aren't always knitted into the sweaters; she's a fan of felting wool, drawing designs on it, cutting them out, and applying them directly.

Like a lot of Icelanders, though, she has an extremely practical view of the lopi and doesn't put much mythology into it. "I'm glad the lopi's become so popular," she tells us. "It means the farmers will sell more wool, and it's been hard on them lately."

Palla shows us a baby sweater she's made in her Faroese style. It's got a honeycombed, 3D quality. Joan asks detailed questions about how the stitches are done, which Palla seems delighted to answer.

Back in 2000, Palla started a co-op with about a hundred other women in Búðardalur. They opened a store that sells hand-knitted items and shares the profits. Each of the members has to spend time working in the store, though they're exempted from doing that once they reach the age of 70; after the younger knitters pick up their hours.

"It's made us all a lot closer," she says. "These are women I never would have met otherwise. And for the past twenty years, we've gotten together and knitted and talked." Do they talk about knitting techniques? Joan asks. "No," she says, "not really."

Even at 91, Palla may have a whole lifetime of knitting ahead of her. She is the oldest child of the last Icelander born in the 19th century. Her mother, Sólveig Pálsdóttir, was born in 1879 and lived to be 109 years old. Each year toward the end of her life, she appeared in the local newspaper, celebrating her birthday and conspicuously knitting.

Eyþór in a fog bank. Lopi by Palla.

Driving back, we hit a fog bank like a brick wall. Suddenly the visibility goes to 20 or 30 feet (6 or 9 m). Eyþór slows down to a crawl, and I suggest he pull over so I can take some photos in the fog.

I open the trunk to get my camera out and spot a dark brown and white lopi balled up in the corner. "I thought you didn't have one of these?" I say, accusatorially, as though I'd just found drugs in a coat pocket.

"Oh!" he says, as though I'd just pointed out a live rabbit in his trunk. "I borrowed that from my mother for a costume party where you had to arrive in a wool jumper. I should have shown it to Palla. She probably made it." He puts it on, and I snap a couple of photos. He looks like a Harry Potter character. There's something really special about this garment, this process, this life, that threads through Palla with her memories of turf houses and stranded sailors and Eyþór with his robotics team and microfiber polar fleece— something that ties one bit of Iceland to all the other bits of Iceland and that keeps all the parts from flying away if something breaks, if something changes. We all wander around in the fog for a while, snapping photos and marveling, until it starts to clear and we get back on the road.

As we roll back into Reykjavik, we thank Eyþór profusely for the experience.

"Not at all," he says. "It was my pleasure. Without this I never would have learned about that part of her life, which is so important to her, so I'm very grateful for the experience."

How can you not like this guy?

On our way back, we get a message from Alon and Arwin. Alon's won second place in the race up north and is heading back with a trophy to return the rental car, pick up the RV, and find us. They'll be here tomorrow.

"The race directions were really weird," he tells us. "It was like 'run that way, keep the river to your left until you get to a bridge, then cross the bridge and run toward the tallest hill.'" He led the pack until the terrain got really tough, when the eventual winner shot ahead like a rabbit and vanished.

Adventure: Reykjavik Is a 24-Hour Party

Back in Reykjavik, Eyþór suggests that we go to Mál og Menning, a large bookstore that's also a café and a bar. Though it's 10 o'clock at night, the sun is still shining brightly. Mál og Menning is packed with used books and people breakdancing to techno music. It's like the bar from a movie where the hero goes to a place where all the cool kids are. Upstairs we spy Smari McCarthy, a member of the Icelandic Parliament, founder of the Pirate Party (no kidding), one of ten members representing the South constituency, which is one of six districts in Iceland. He's holding court at a large table surrounded by a half-dozen people. He waves at Eyþór, because everybody in Reykjavik knows everybody, and we go over.

"Can you just hang out at a bar without security guards?" we ask. "It's fine!" he says. "Iceland's not like that." Before becoming a politician, Smari was the chief technologist for OCCRP, the Organized Crime and Corruption Reporting Project, where he created an open-source database for combating organized crime. "I'm only one of two politicians in Iceland who got elected and got fewer death threats," he laughs over the din. He immediately waves some other people over to the table. "This is Halla," he says. "Her family lives in the south, and they've designed lopis for years. You should talk to her."

The beers are large but expensive. We pay 1,400 króna each (about 12 dollars), and from our perch on the second floor, we can look down onto the crowd of dancers. Eyþór's girlfriend, Margrét, shows up. She's an actress, producer, and director. Pretty soon after, Mikael wanders in and sits down at the table with us. It takes about 20 minutes before he and Margrét realize they were in a movie together where they played Vikings. She digs out a photo on her cell phone, showing the two of them covered in makeup and gore and waving axes. "I think it comes out next year!" Margrét says, leaning close. The music gets loud, more people show up in waves, and the party rolls out into the street. It's 2 a.m., but the sun is still out, and the streets are packed with people. We've lost Eyþór and Smari, pushed away by the tide, but Mikael's still with us. Tourists zoom by

Mál og Menning: a bookstore, a nightclub, a bar, and—we find out later—a publisher. Joan and Eyþór and Smari are visible way in the back, on the second floor.

Mikael wearing the Everywhere Sweater, and the party that never ends.

on scooters, and there's a line 50 people long to get into Prikið, which is apparently not the quiet spot we'd come to know it to be during the day. People wave from rooftops. The whole thing feels like Wildwood, New Jersey, at the height of the summer, where the party is a breathing miasma that hangs in the air, and tendrils of fragmented, half-remembered yesterdays reach out lazily and lay themselves across you and everything seems like it's important but that you can't possibly hold on to enough of it.

I find myself talking with Madhav, the first mate on a container ship that's docked in the harbor somewhere. He's from India, and this is his 26th visit to Reykjavik. He's got long hair and a leather jacket and punctuates every sentence with a violent motion of a beer glass that he appears to have stolen from the bar and from which he never seems to spill a drop, despite how animated he becomes. It feels like everybody on the street looks like some sort of rock star, but it may be the bottle of gin someone's passing around that gives that impression. Madhav tells me that the most difficult part about working on a container ship isn't surviving the storms without getting seasick, but

figuring out the logistics of packing and unpacking the containers. This is, not unnaturally, called *container logistics*. It used to be primarily done by people, but now it's almost entirely automated. Computers figure out in what order the containers need to be stacked in for the most efficient transport, which also needs to include things like weight-balancing the ship to keep it from rolling too much. Computers are particularly good at this. And in fact, he tells me, in a lot of ports, almost everything is automated. Computers drive autonomous vehicles and cranes that tirelessly and without complaint lift containers from the ship and place them on autonomous, computer-driven terminal trucks that cart them off to autonomous computer-driven stacker cranes that load them onto a train or a truck—and while all this is happening, the crew is out getting drunk.

I ask if they've ever lost a container.

"Oh, of course," he says. "Thousands of containers fall overboard every year. It's not a perfect system."

At 3 a.m., we're just too tired to keep it up any longer. Tomorrow we start out on our adventure around the Ring Road. Tomorrow the volcano awaits.

Adventure: Volcano

Six months ago, on February 24, 2020, I got a text message from Kiddi, saying, "You're missing out on an Icelandic experience right now! We had four pretty big earthquakes over the space of about five to eight minutes!" This was followed later by a video of his apartment shaking that also went viral on Twitter. Icelandic mythology says that earthquakes are caused by the god Loki shifting beneath the earth, but everybody really suspected it was something different than that. A month later, Kiddi texted again—just one word: "Eruption!"

There was a sort-of joke going around Iceland in those months, revolving around the words *eldgos*, meaning "volcanic eruption"; *held*, "thought"; and then the portmanteau *heldgos*, which translates literally as "thought eruption" but vernacularly as "the anticipation of an eruption"—just waiting for something to blow up and not knowing how it's going to be.

There are 120 volcanoes in Iceland, and there's usually a big eruption about every three years, though things have been quiet lately (at the time of this writing). The last big eruption was Eyjafjallajökull in April 2010, which spewed ash into the atmosphere, shutting down air traffic around the world as well as melting the glacier above it and causing major flooding. The eruption everybody is expecting, and dreading, is Katla in the south, which has erupted with obsessive regularity every 20 to 90 years or so for the past six centuries and is well overdue for a big, messy explosion that everybody's talking about but nobody wants to think about.

This time, though, it wasn't Katla; rather, the eruption was a volcano known as Fagradalsfjall in Geldingadalur on the Rekjanes Peninsula, just a few miles away from Reykjavik and even closer to Keflavik, making it perfectly suited for someone who wanted to visit the Blue Lagoon and a volcano

Kyle and Joan. Kyle is wearing the Everywhere Sweater (cardigan) and Joan is wearing the Lakeside Lopapeysa and the Hot Springs Hat. Behind-the-scenes photo by Alon Abramson.

and then go home. This eruption presented itself first as a single cone, with magma spewing magnificently from a hole in the ground that grew day by day. "It's kind of a perfect tourist volcano," Kiddi told us. "It's in the middle of nowhere, and it's just slowly oozing magma." Before this, Fagradalsfjall had been dormant for 6,000 years.

Alon and Arwin arrive with a gigantic mobile home, into which we settle and claim our spots, stow our bags, and marvel at all the conveniences. A bathroom! A fridge! A kitchen! Beds! How could we not have the most luxurious time? The future stretches out before us like unwritten pages of joy.

We drive to Grindavik, just 30 miles (52 km) away, and find that a dirt parking lot has been constructed on the side of the road and it's filled with 60 or 70 cars, camper vans, and mobile homes. If this were the United States, there would also be someone charging $45 to park. But being Iceland, no such thing is being done. We'd heard conflicting reports on what was ahead. Eyþór said it was an easy walk, maybe a half hour. Rebekka, who's been photographing Fagradalsfjall with a drone for months now, said it was about an hour to the volcano.

Kiddi's first photos showed himself and Guðný at the base of a small cone that looked a bit like the model of Devil's Tower from *Close Encounters*. It was a pretty cute volcano, but a lot has happened in the last six months, and the volcano has drastically changed both its appearance and the landscape, filling the Natthagi Valley and flowing over the sides of a number of hills, creating a sheet of lava that spreads for miles. The path that Eyþór walked probably doesn't exist anymore, and the cone now seems to be hundreds of feet high.

We walk about a mile before we see the farthest extension of the lava, which extends like a lake, probably a mile (1.6 km) long and a half mile (0.8 km) wide, rolling black, in some places still steaming and in others very cool. Walking along the sides, you can occasionally feel heat emanating from it. The lava, where it's cooled, is very fragile, and kicking it will shatter hundreds of small, lima bean-sized pieces off. We stand around and take photos, wondering if we should get all of our gear out before someone says, *Let's keep walking toward the volcano. This may not seem so impressive a mile from now.* And sure enough, even though this might be the most impressive

Through the mist, Trillian in the Everywhere Sweater and Alon in the Puffin Sweater.

Our first glimpse of Fagradalsfjall, erupting in the distance. Arwin in the Icelandic Horse Sweater, Alon in the Puffin Sweater, Trillian in the Everywhere Sweater, Joan in the Lakeside Lopapeysa.

thing that I've ever seen, as we climb the first of several very, very substantial hills, we can see a red glow off in the distance, still several miles away—the sky being lit up by magma; the volcano. It's an awe-inspiring sight. As we continue, getting higher and closer, we literally ascend into a cloud, and everything goes dark. We can only see a few hundred feet around us. The valley below has vanished. Occasionally the fog thins ahead, and the sky glows orange.

The walk is a lot longer than we'd expected. An hour and a half later, we still seem to be about three-quarters of a mile away. In the distance, the volcano sounds like the sea, but with waves of lava crashing into one another. We sit on the side of a hill and watch it for about half an hour. Occasionally there are other people. Some pass us, and some we see sitting on rocks just staring out into the distance. Everyone is having their very profound experience, feeling so, so tiny in

nature, and understanding, maybe just a little bit, what we'd learned in geology class years ago about how the earth is composed. I think back to that word, *heldgos*—anticipating an eruption. This is what everybody was going through between the earthquakes and the first squirt of lava out in Geldingadalir—the anticipation that something was happening, but not knowing exactly what it was going to be. Would it be catastrophic? Would it boil up in the center of Reykjavik? Would it bury the city in ash? In lava? Would there be a cacophonous explosion? Would homes be destroyed? Ultimately, you can either get on a plane and head to Denmark or you can go about your business, and this is what people in a lot of places do every day. But it's a powerful sword to have to live beneath: the realization that any time it wants, the very land you live on can rise up and destroy you, and there's not much you can do about it. *Which is not to say there is*

At the volcano. Trillian in the Everywhere Sweater, Arwin in the Icelandic Horse Sweater, and Alon in the Puffin Sweater.

nothing you can do about it. Sometimes there is. Back in 1973, the Eldfell volcano on the island of Vestmannaeyjar erupted, disgorging a flow of lava headed straight for the town of Heimaey, home of some 4,500 people. Half the town was destroyed, but not before physicist Þorbjörn Sigurgeirsson got the idea of spraying the lava with seawater to cool it in some places but not others. This created barriers that then directed the rest of the flow into the ocean and spared the remainder of the town—which, due to the ground itself being lava, increased in size by almost exactly one-third.

If Fagradalsfjall eventually threatens Grindavik, there will be an awful lot of warning, and a lot of valleys will get filled with lava first. That's not an impossible scenario. There are lava fields in Iceland more than 310 miles (500 km) square.

All this dances through our minds while the wind whips around us and it gets very cold. We put on all the lopis that we have and try to get closer. Eventually it appears that the way before

us is cut off with molten rock. There is no way around it; there is no carefully constructed path over it. This is not the intersection of humans and nature, carefully curated like you might see in a geothermal area. This is nature just doing whatever it wants and people being as they are: ants running toward a particularly enticing bread crumb.

Eventually we realize that it is over, that we've come this way and experienced this marvelous thing that people will ask us about and that we'll never be able to explain exactly, but it's time to go home. The trip back takes about an hour and a half over the same rocky terrain up and down. I manage fairly well, but coming down that big first hill (now the last big hill), I fall and tear my elbow open. I can't see what it looks like, but there's definitely blood, and I ask if it looks like it'll leave a scar, because a volcano scar sounds like a cool thing to have.

We camp at Grindavik, but we arrive late and get up early, so there's not much to see.

Adventure: Hestaland—A Horse Farm Where You Can Stay

The next morning, we drive north along Route 1 to Hestaland, an equine retreat in Borgarnes where people can come and spend a week or two doing horse-riding tours and staying at the well-appointed guest house. Hestaland is owned by Guðmar Þór Pétursson, who's been working with horses for 30 years, and his wife, Christina, whom he met on a Southwest Airlines flight between Kentucky and Chicago. Christina took advantage of Southwest's open seating to plop herself next to someone who seemed interesting, and now she lives in Iceland, speaks the language, and works with horses every day. Hestaland paired up with author Nancy Mary Brown, an expert on Viking history, to create a series of Saga tours that combine horseback riding with Icelandic history. At the moment, Christina's sister, Ali, is visiting from the United States with her husband, Nick, to check on a house that they bought, sight unseen, during the COVID lockdown.

The farm is bustling with people and animals. Guðmar, Christina, and their daughter Embla are getting ready for an Icelandic horse festival next week, and because of that, their farm is boarding a bunch of out-of-town horses. Despite the busy time of year, we are greeted enthusiastically, fed, and given a tour by Embla.

"Icelandic horses have a unique temperament," Guðmar tells us. "They're smart and trusting and well-tempered. They come in all colors except appaloosa." Unlike American horses, which are bred for specialization, there's only one breed of Icelandic horse. Horses for riding or hauling or farmwork are all the same.

"A horse," Guðmar says, "will always react as a horse. And when you get a horse, you have no idea what that horse has been through. Horses learn

Hestaland. Ali and Joan wearing Lakeside Lopapeysas, August in the Child Puffin Sweater, Kyle in the Everywhere Cardigan, Embla in the Icelandic Horse Sweater, Arwin holding a light. Photo by Trillian Stars.

Ali wearing the Lakeside Lopapeysa.

by reacting, and if a horse has been rewarded for something or punished for something and it's reinforced for years, then that horse will do things based on those former experiences, but a horse is always honest. We say in Iceland that a horse comes to the door the way they are dressed—meaning they don't try to fool you; they tell you exactly who they are."

Today, Embla is riding a new horse that has its own ideas about what they're going to do—specifically *not* going into the frigid river. But however stubborn the horse is, Embla is more resolute. This is a test of wills that she absolutely refuses to back down from, and within an hour, they're traveling back and forth across the water, up and over rocks and back, splashing joyfully.

We drive north from Hestaland through green valleys speckled with sheets of yellow flowers, find a campsite behind a Lutheran church with a small cemetery, and get settled for the night.

Adventure: Illugastaðir—The Land of Seals and Ghosts

The itinerary just said "seals and ghosts?" with a dot on the map far to the north. They both sounded intriguing, especially the ghosts. Further investigation into this revealed that seals often hang out on the shores doing seal things and that this was also the spot of Iceland's last execution. Iceland is a pretty progressive place, and they got rid of their death penalty long ago. The last execution was in 1830, while they were still part of Denmark, and even that was after a 40-year lull. The story of these executions and the crimes that precipitated them have often been retold: it is the subject of Egill Eðvarðsson's 1995 Icelandic film *Agnes* and, more recently, it appears in the best-selling novel *Burial Rites*, by the Australian novelist Hanna Kent. Both tell the story of a mysterious pair of violent murders and the trial and eventual execution of a man and a woman, Friðrik Sigurðsson and Agnes Magnúsdóttir, who may have had varying degrees of culpability. While some of the story is hazy, a lot was written down at the time in excruciating, bureaucratic detail. What we do know is that on March 14, 1828, Nathan Ketilsson, a self-professed wizard, and his ne'er-do-well friend, Pétur Jónsson, died in a fire in a farmhouse. Further investigation showed that both bodies also possessed a number of stab wounds. Three people were arrested, interrogated, and tried, and two of them, Agnes and Friðrik, were beheaded.

The murder site and the execution site are both relatively accessible. The murder site is up Route 711, a gravel road dotted with periodic signs pointing out scenic vistas and asking you to complain about the state of the road on social media (not kidding). The execution site is conveniently located right off the Ring Road.

The farmhouse is gone (having been burned down during the murder), but Nathan's workshop, where he made his various healing tinctures, is more or less still there in the form of some low fieldstone walls along the shore. It's picturesque.

Þrístapar, the execution site, is in the middle of a farmer's field, surrounded by goats, who pause from eating grass and look up suspiciously as we walk past, and horses, who couldn't seem to care less. Þrístapar means "three hills," and while there are three hills in a row, there are also literally hundreds more mounds splatted around the area like so many cow pies. It might just as well be called "ten hills." The site is undergoing some renovation—possibly from the attention drawn to it by the book and the movie(s)—in the form of a very nice path being installed, along with a series of stone markers that tell the story in short increments as you approach the site, moving toward the inevitable outcome, and then more stones with thoughts for reflection on your way back.

Agnes and Friðrik were originally buried on the spot of the execution (after their heads were displayed on pikes for some period of time to serve as a disincentive to the townspeople), but in 1934 they were disinterred and reburied in a churchyard.

According to local legend, Agnes's ghost visited a Reykjavik psychic in 1932 and asked that her head be reunited with her body, leaving explicit instructions as to where her head might be found. When people with shovels were dispatched, they quickly found the remains and reinterred them at Tjörn Church on the Vatnsnes Peninsula. None of my attempts to find primary sources for the psychic story has been successful, though there are headstones at Tjörn. Presumably something is buried there, but I can't find any records of the 1932 disinterment.

One thing that's remarkable about this story is just how much of it is so thoroughly documented. Novelist Hanna Kent scoured the National Archives of Iceland, Þjóðskjalasafn Íslands (which is on the western edge of Reykjavik on Laugavegur 162, down the street from a couple of thrift stores where you might find a nice lopi). There she found the letters and papers of district commissioner Björn Blöndal, who was in charge of the execution, and who wrote back and forth with officials in Denmark with great regularity and detail. The archives include a five-page missive from G. Johnson, secretary to the King of Denmark, detailing exactly how the execution would proceed, who must attend, where they would stand, what would happen to the bodies (buried "on the spot without ceremony, in white untreated wood") and the heads ("set upon two stakes"), who has to pay to have the axe made (Iceland) and what exactly will happen to it after the execution (it had to be returned to Copenhagen at the event's end, though it's back in Iceland right now at the National Museum). While these things are recorded and preserved with a level of ministerial beadledom that is, I suppose, produced as a byproduct of 100% literacy, long inhospitable winters, and a devastating remoteness, much of the human aspect is left completely to your imagination. Was Agnes a murderer or a wronged woman? What were her final thoughts in the last days? Climb the three hills at Tristapar like she did in 1830; put on your lopi at the top of the hill, because it's cold; and as you look out onto the mountains and fields, which look now just as they did then, see what you feel in your heart.

The roads here are a bit bumpy, and at times it feels like we're riding through a gauntlet where people are firing pellet guns at us nonstop. There are frequent bangs and pings as gravel ricochets from the sides of the vehicle. I try to remember what exactly the insurance card said about gravel damage and am somewhere lost in contemplation of this when there is a particularly loud *bang!* and I see something flash past the window.

"I think a pillow might have fallen out the window!" I say, but nobody's listening. Finally, I climb up into the loft to see what's going on and notice that while all the pillows are there in the loft bed, the entire window is gone, leaving just a hole to the outside through which a fierce wind is howling.

"The window's gone," I say, climbing back down. There's some discussion, and we decide to turn around and look for it, but the Ring Road, in its entirety, is a pencil-narrow two lanes with no shoulder and very few turnoffs. A truck of turnips overturning in the right place could shut the whole country down for days. Finally, we find a place to turn around, but by then it's been so long, nobody really remembers where we were when the window flew off.

I call the RV company and tell them what happened. The woman on the other end of the phone seems concerned but not surprised. They ask where we are. "Dalvik," I say. "Somewhere near Dalvik."

"Very good!" she replies cheerfully. "We have a station in Akureyri. Stop by there, and have them take a look at it."

Akureyri is Iceland's sixth-largest town. It stands in for the Big City in all the crime novels about the remote North. People are always getting carted off to the hospital in Akureyri, or the lab, or some missing piece of equipment is being shuttled in from there. I'm excited to see it. But first we camp in Dalvik.

Camping, Whale Watching

Dalvik is surrounded by mountains. I get out a map and try to find out what their names are, but I can't figure it out. They're huge, though, looming up over everything. I'm from Pennsylvania, where we have really old mountains. They don't have peaks—they're just rolls—and they're not this high, so I spend a lot of time staring up at these. The campground is nice. The bathrooms are a bit luxurious, and the common area is nice, though the Wi-Fi signal drops off so precipitously in relation to it that we pack up and move 40 feet to get better reception. I'm paranoid about losing photos, so I'm trying to upload images every night. I decide to edit photos and write in my diary, and everyone else opts to go whale watching in the Eyjafjörður fjord.

Trillian looking for seals or ghosts at the site of Natan Ketilsson's murder wearing the Waiting Cape and the Vik Dress

Adventure: Lopi Thrifting in the Rauði Krossinn

After everyone else comes back, excited and filled with stories of humpback whales popping up right next to the boat, we leave the campsite in search of a Bonus supermarket. A joyous hue and cry come up when someone sights a Rauði Krossinn, "Red Cross," Iceland's national thrift store. There's one in most of the larger towns (mainly scattered on the west coast), and they're a pretty good place to find inexpensive lopi sweaters. True to form, this one has two racks of lopis, one in adult and the other in children's sizes, each knitted by an authentic Icelandic grandmother and abandoned to a resale store by a callous relative. While there are a lot of them, they were indeed knitted by authentic Icelandic grandmothers—who may be a lot like your own grandmother, and many of them have the eye-jarring color schemes of whatever garish acrylic yarn was in the discount rack at the yarn store, including glittery yarns woven with tinsel spun into them, some with bejeweled buttons. So be prepared to spend a lot of time across a number of stores looking for the perfect secondhand lopi. Also, be forewarned that in the bigger towns with larger tourist populations, the sweaters will cost more. But if you're touring the country and you're not in a hurry, you can get a lopi for 30 to 50 percent of the price of a new one by checking out the Red Cross. Also check online before going, because many of them have very limited hours. One by one, squeals of delight go up from everyone in our group as they find a lopi that both looks beautiful and fits. Everybody but me, that is. I make a mental note to get knitting.

Joan wearing Hot Springs the Hot and Lakeside Lopapeysa while whale watching in Dalvik. Photo by Trillian Stars.

Whale watching in Dalvik. Photo by Alon Abramson.

Hot Tub Party

Every town in Iceland has a public "swimming pool"; some are what Americans traditionally think of as swimming pools, but others are just a hot tub or series of hot tubs. If you're a runner and looking to get in some kilometers with some Icelanders, a lot of local running clubs will use the swimming pools as a meetup spot for weekly runs. For somewhere between 650 and 1,000 króna, you can get admission to the pool and spend the morning or the afternoon (or all day, if you'd like) luxuriating in bathtub-temperature water or switching between the hot tub and the cold tub for a bracing experience. The swimming pool at Dalvik is like nothing we've ever seen before in Iceland. It's like a theme park, sporting three hot tubs of varying temperatures, a cold tank, an Olympic-sized swimming pool, and two giant water slides, as well as incredible vistas. We decide to stay an extra day in Dalvik just lounging around. This is a benefit of scheduling your trip loosely.

The campground at Dalvik is quiet and beautiful and 100 yards from a really wonderful waterpark.

Akureyri

We arrive in Akureyri, which, despite having an airport and being the big city of the north, is only about two miles across at the widest, housing some 18,000 people. We find the RV place, and I go in and explain our plight. One by one, everyone wanders outside to look at the damage, walk around the RV, and make sour faces. They don't have a new window, but they'll fix it up, they promise. It'll take about a half hour. We walk to a nearby coffee shop, and I have a pretty nice cup of coffee that I squeeze out from a thermos myself, and we sit down and plan the day. I notice that the signs aren't in English and Icelandic anymore—they're just in Icelandic, so I have to use Google translate to figure out which restroom to use.

This is made slightly more difficult by the fact that the bathrooms aren't labeled "Men's" and "Women's" but "Eldfjall" and "Jökull" ("volcanoes" and "glaciers"), and it takes me frantic minutes of googling before I make a terrified random guess and am relieved to see a urinal instead of someone screaming at me.

We finish our coffee and wander back to the RV place, where they've taped up the window with plastic and about two rolls of duct tape. "That should last forever!" the satisfied repair person says, hands on hips, looking up at his handiwork. It looks like he's done this before.

After we leave, I realize that I failed to take a single photo.

Trillian in the Everywhere Sweater, contemplating the massive lava field produced by the Fagradalsfjall Volcano.

Behind the scenes: Trillian being cooked for a photo in the Adventure Sweater. Joan, Arwin, and Alon, holding lights.

Adventure: Got Cave?

The next day, we meet Hjördís at Vogafjós café at Lake Mývatn, 81 miles (130 km) from Dalvik. Vogafjós is a wide, charming restaurant and coffee shop that reminds me of a ski lodge more than anything else. Wide windows on one wall look out onto a field of sleeping cows and the lake itself, and along the other wall, equally wide windows look into a dairy barn, where cows are being milked. We order coffee and sit down on plush sofas and relax. Hjördís is the sister of Kiddi's best friend from school—they used to play in a band together, but now her brother is the chief technical officer for the video game company 1939 Games, creators of the popular game *Kards*. Hjördís suggests that we go to Grjótagjá Cave, where Jon Snow and Ygritte hooked up in *Game of Thrones* season 3, episode 5, "Kissed by Fire." A lot of *Game of Thrones* was filmed in Iceland, much to the delight of the tourism industry and the horror of the locals.

Grjótagijá Cave used to be open to the public, but after the TV show it became swiftly swamped by foreigners trying to live out their King in the North dreams and creating a nuisance, so the townspeople gated the cave—or rather, one of the caves. Hjördís points out that there are two caves, known as the "men's" cave and the "women's" cave (she also tells us it's traditional to bathe in the nude here). Continual volcanic activity in the 1970s and 1980s brought magma closer to the surface and raised the temperature of the water in the caves to more than 120 degrees F (49 C)—too hot for bathing—but recently the temperature in the women's cave has come down. Because it's not terribly useful for bathing, the people of Mývatn have left the men's cave open so visitors can stop in and have a look (and as we arrived, a tourist in a bathing suit and flip-flops was running toward the mouth of the cave, intent on parboiling himself for an Instagram photo).

The caves are in the shadow of Hverfjall, an enormous volcanic crater a kilometer across, formed 2500 BP by an enormous volcanic

Cows outside Vogafjós. This is your view if you sit on the deck. It's a pretty nice view.

explosion. We learn here that geologists use "BP," "before the present," in dating things. It may seem that "the present" is a really slippery slope to use in science because it changes with each day, but when we started setting off nuclear bombs in the 1940s, we screwed up the efficacy of radio carbon dating by adding all sorts of radiation to the air. There are two trails that lead up to the rim of Hverfjall, and then the walk along it is spectacular.

When we get to the women's cave, we find that the gate is unlocked. Another Mývatn local is using it. Hjördís lets us know they probably won't be long because the water, while cooler than in the other cave, is still very hot, and people don't stay in it for long. True enough, they come out shortly, red from head to toe and very relaxed looking. Hjördís leads us in, and we photograph a sweater. About 15 minutes in the water is all I can take. It feels wonderful and magical, but it makes me desperately want to go to sleep.

We sit on the rocks for a while and talk, occasionally jumping back in for 60 seconds or so. When the photos are done, we clamber out and head back to Vogafjós for drinks and snacks on the back patio. It's unseasonably warm right now, and the locals are spending as much time outside as possible. Hjördís's husband stops by on the way into work. He's an emergency airplane pilot out of Akureyri, where he flies people with serious medical emergencies, usually to the hospital in Reykjavik. I ask him if it's a lot of tourists, and he answers that he's actually surprised how few tourists need to be evacuated to Reykjavik, considering how many of them there are in the area. Mostly it's Icelanders with all sorts of medical needs, from accidents to heart attacks. The flight itself takes about 40 minutes.

Next, we stop at Dyngjan Handverk Mývatnssveit, which is a co-op of about 60 women (including Hjördís's frænka, Margrét) who sell

they'd be unable to identify a lopi made in the '60s, '70s, or '80s from one made today. The designs are pretty timeless.

What do they know about the very first lopi? We want to know about its origins. On this topic, they're all pretty sure Auður Sveinsdóttir Laxness designed it, probably for Álafoss, and published it, probably not in a magazine but on a single sheet. Margrét runs into the back and comes out with a sweater made from the pattern they think was probably the first, which contains an eight-petaled rose—the *dryas octopetala*—an arctic alpine flower that grows in large colonies across Iceland.[1] This flower is on the lopi that I got during my last visit to Iceland, and I'd always mistaken it for a snowflake. I also discover that in 1994, Mál og menning, a publisher with a vague though complex relationship with the bookstore/bar/hip-hop party palace of the same name that Eyþór took us to, came out with an edition of *Icelandic Sjónabók*, an 18th-century collection of Icelandic designs that has been mined for quilts, needlepoints, and sweaters ever since. It's out of print at the moment, and the cheapest copy I can find is 225 euros online.

Joan talks technique with Margrét at the Dyngjan Handverk Mývatnssveit.

handcrafts. Piles of luxurious lopi sweaters are the centerpiece of the small, bustling shop, which ingests and disgorges tourists at a surprising rate that keeps us from standing too close to the door. There are three women working there now. One is knitting a hat from a plate of lopi, and she shows us how she plucks a strand from the inside and pairs it with the one on the outside.

We ask Margrét if she remembers her first lopi— and she does. Her mother taught her to knit, and she made a lopi dress that included her initials on the hip, something that turned out to be far more difficult than she'd initially imagined. That bit of innovation was surprisingly unique, though. Apart from the colors and the use of zippers instead of buttons, all three women are fairly certain that

1. Later I ask Ásdís Jóelsdóttir about this, hoping she may have a copy of the pattern. She's not heard this story and is skeptical. She's looked through a lot of old archives and tells us the first pattern from Álafoss was by Aðalheiður and wasn't printed until 1961, and by that time people had been trading patterns informally for a while. Though she won at least one contest sponsored by them, no one's found any evidence that Auður ever actually designed anything for Álafoss. Which just shows how difficult it is to pin down the origins of this garment, even among people who were part of its early formation.

The Mývatn Geothermal Area.

Adventure: Námafjall Hverir, the Mývatn Geothermal Area

On the way from Mývatn to the East Fjords, we pass right by Námafjall Hverir, the Mývatn Geothermal Area, and although I'm all geothermal-ed out, everybody else wants to stop. We pull into a wide, mostly empty dirt parking lot that smells like rotting eggs in front of a fan, and everybody piles out while I edit cave photos. After about 20 minutes, I finish tagging everything (an important part of photography is adding metadata to the images so you can later tell where they were taken and who was in them). Nobody's back yet, so I open the door to the RV, and a cloud of hideous-smelling steam billows in, like I've opened the door to Satan's bathroom. Around us is a vast expanse of fumaroles, belching smoke (in fact, the root of the word *fumarole* is the Latin word *fumus*, from which we also get "fumes") as well as bubbling mud pots. Since 1969, Icelanders have used this heat source to drive the nearby Bjarnarflag geothermal power plant, which produces 18 billion watt-hours per year. As power stations go, Bjarnarflag is pretty small, a collection of five or six diminutive buildings the size of tiny houses connected by a series of pipes. Apart from electricity, Bjarnarflag provides hot water to the locals and dumps its wastewater into the Mývatn nature baths (exactly as the Blue Lagoon is filled by the wastewater from the Svartsengi power station). This is a remarkable feat. Coming as I do from Pennsylvania, where it's really hard to plan a family vacation around coal or nuclear power plants, the idea that the most toxic by-product of your energy production is warm water that's perfect for bathing in is mind blowing.

Here at Námafjall Hverir, a smattering of tourists wander across the orange landscape, guided mostly by thin ropes that do nothing but suggest people not step over them to fall into broiling pits of mud or deep holes belching fumes. It seems, at the very least, uninspired to say that Námafjall Hverir looks like another planet, but it certainly doesn't look much like this planet. Pools of mud are literally boiling, mineral deposits from deep within the earth have collected here, changing the colors of the surface, and steam spews from fissures and holes. On top of that, it's not terribly crowded, and there's an enormous amount of space to wander around in.

Möðrudalur: The Farm at the Top of the World

While planning our itinerary, someone put a pin in Möðrudalur, which advertises itself as the highest working farm in Iceland (1,353 feet [469 m] above sea level) and an out-of-the-way place that has some space available for camping. It seemed like a quiet spot where I might sit and work on photographs and knit, peacefully far from the cares of the world, and perhaps see an intermittent, faraway farmer, tooling by on an ancient tractor, who might pause to wave at me because I was probably the only human being he'd seen that year. It sounded pretty idyllic, but it wasn't, really.

Möðrudalur, which among its other honorifics also boasts the coldest temperature ever recorded in Iceland, −38.0°C (−36.4°F), back in 1918,[1] is off the Ring Road by some 12.5 miles (20 km). During this drive, it sounds like the RV is being machine-gunned by an incredibly well-equipped army, and nobody is able to think a coherent thought. And while it might have been out of the way, it seems that every other American in Iceland found the same tourist brochure, because the place is packed with my countrymen—talking loudly, wandering around shirtless, attempting to parallel-park their RVs on listing hills, setting up tents and pop-up trailers, hanging their laundry out—and an entire circus of children is running this way and that, shouting and chasing barn cats. The common area, which I'd become so used to at every campground, is largely nonexistent, replaced by a small, Disney-like village of sod-roofed log buildings, one promising an as-yet-unfinished Volcano Museum, one housing men's and women's pay toilets (100 ISK, please), and one with a restaurant that offers a 2,400 ISK vegetable soup as well as postcards and various knickknacks and also handles the checking in. Midges are there in full force, flying up noses, in ears, and every which way. (Mývatn means "lake of midges" but we'd somehow avoided them thus far.) There are some really scenic vistas as well as a church that performs services for tourists and the beginnings of a farm-equipment museum tucked along a boardwalk path. Möðrudalur is buzzing with activity, especially in the lobby of the restaurant and gift shop, which seems to be the only place anybody can get a cell phone signal. This does cause me to linger there for a half hour, eavesdropping on Americans calling home to complain about the midges and ask what time it is back wherever they came from.

The campground's main redeeming quality is the goats wandering around and climbing into any opened shelter looking for hugs and handouts. I spend an inordinate amount of time snuggling them and giving them all our vegetable scraps. Early the next morning, I get up before anyone else, gather my things, and step outside to find myself the only human being yet roused. I breathe in the fresh air, as well as a few midges, and find a picnic table in the shade (the sun having been up since April), where I am immediately befriended by all the goats, who come wandering over hoping I have either a pocketful of zucchini or the time to scratch them behind the ears.

I divide my time between working on photos, knitting my sweater, and petting the goats. For two hours, I have the entire world to myself before Joan comes wandering up the hill with a pot of coffee and we plan the day.

Trillian snuggling a goat in her thrift store lopi.

1. Remember Margrét Sigurðardóttir and Gunnvör Magnúsdóttir, who first knit with lopi because it was so cold and they needed sweaters fast? This was the same winter. https://www.vedur.is/vedur/frodleikur/greinar/nr/1042.

Djúpivogur, looking into the fjord, Berufjörður.

Djúpivogur

The East Fjords, which someone later calls "the Florida of Iceland" because of its warmer weather, is where Kiddi has suggested we could visit a sheep farm where his father works, but it turns out his father is on his way to Reykjavik to get an auto part repaired. So instead, we go to Djúpivogur, a fishing village of about 400 residents, and avail ourselves of the indoor swimming pool. I could really get used to a daily soak in the hot tub. There are three tubs here, once again of varying temperatures, as well as an Olympic-sized pool (I imagine that I will get letters saying, *You keep saying this word* Olympic *but you do not know what it means*)—or at least a really large pool with lanes and diving platforms. It also sports an outdoor area (currently closed). We move leisurely between the various temperatures while a bunch of Icelanders do the same. Joan and I have a lot of work to do, taking close-ups of all the sweaters and also photos of new pieces that she's made along the way. She's continually inspired by

the people and things we see and bangs out a new piece almost daily. The clicking of her needles from the back of the RV is the melody of the soundtrack of gravel pelting the side of our mobile home. We set up a photo studio on a picnic table by the sinks at the campground and go about checking off what needs to be photographed and what has been photographed. Joan's arrived with three suitcases of sweaters, and she's been handing them out to people along the way after we're sure we have the right image. It's her goal to have three empty suitcases by the time we get back to Reykjavik.

The campground at Djúpivogur is fairly small but nice; it's located in a small valley buffered by tiny trees on two sides, an expanse of grassland on the third, and a view of the nearby harbor on the last. Joan and I finish the close-ups, and we all go off to bed.

In the morning before we leave, Trillian and I wander around the town and then down to the harbor to look at the commercial fishing boats. Djúpivogur is particularly well located for fishing, and it doesn't take the boats long to get into rich fishing areas. About 40 percent of the people in town work for Búlandstindur, a family-run company that focuses primarily on long-line fishing of cod and haddock. Along the docks are a series of photos in an outdoor gallery installation showing people from the area doing things—most of which revolve around fish.

Fishing has been extremely important to Iceland since the very beginning. So important are the fishing grounds in the North Atlantic that Iceland fought three protracted battles with England over them. Dubbed the "cod wars" (Þorskastríðin), they revolved around the English fishing fleet encroaching more and more on Iceland every year as the Brits' deep appreciation for fish and chips met up with European overfishing and an expanding population. From 1958 to 1961, 1972 to 1973, and 1975 to 1976, the Icelandic coast guard, consisting of mostly unarmed boats, fended off first a plethora of fishing trawlers and then, in the advanced stages of the conflict, the actual British navy. Eventually Iceland threatened to leave NATO, and England acquiesced, so valuable were the military assets in and around Iceland—not just the airbase at Keflavik, but the submarine listening posts that made up a valuable portion of the SOSUS network (SOund SUrveillance System) that allows NATO to listen for Soviet submarines coming through the Greenland-Iceland-United Kingdom gap (called GIUK, because the military never met something it didn't need to create an acronym for). The subsequent loss of fish was catastrophic for the British fishing fleet.

We meet Þorgrímur, who's worked on fishing boats since he was 15. For the past dozen years, his advanced skill set in managing fishing boats has put him in great demand, and he's worked all over the world. He gets a little excited when we mention lopapeysas.

"My mom still knits. She's in her late seventies and makes the best sweaters I've ever seen. She sends me, regularly, socks and mittens. So whenever I need something, I just call my mom." He produces a gray, ribbed watch cap from a pocket and puts it on his head. "She made this hat for me, which is my favorite hat. It's cool . . . I think . . . and it's really warm. And she made these." From another pocket he pulls a pair of blue lopi gloves with a running horse and mountain motif. "It astonishes everyone. There's a place called

Skagafjörður; it's a pattern from there, it's very famous for horses. She sends me gloves and mittens whenever I need these things. I don't use the sweater so much anymore . . . not a lot. At sea, the usage of the wool . . . that is probably declining a little bit on the bigger vessels, but on the smaller vessels, when you have to work outside, I would do that. I work now in hot countries mostly, where I don't need such a warm thing. I just came back from the Middle East, and next I'm going to Africa."

But at home, the sweaters still see a lot of use. "I have . . . three or four sweaters," he says, "that I use regularly in the winter. What I use most are scarves and hats and mittens. I've never found anything that keeps me more warm. Sometimes it gets to be thirty below [-22° F] in the wintertime, and the lopi is my weapon of choice."

He's a little sad at what he thinks of some of that tradition going away.

"The new generation, like my kids, they don't want to use it because the material is . . . tickling . . . so they prefer something else. But I think they will grow into it, and they'll start wearing it for cultural pride reasons or grandma pride reasons or something like that," he laughs.

The lopi's success, he points out, is part of its downfall, because people who fish mostly aren't exposed to the same conditions they were 30 or 40 years ago. "On the fishing vessels today," he says, "they are too warm because you work a lot and you sweat a lot, and the sweaters are so hot . . . just too hot." He pauses to specify, "They're too hot to work on a trawler. But on inliners or smaller boats where you have to stand outside, that's where you want one."

And taking this into account, it makes sense that Rebekka's designs and others from the early 2000s were of lighter Léttlopi yarn and included things like zippers, which make it easier for someone mixing fabrics (like an outer waterproof layer or modern microfibers) to regulate their temperature, as the lopi evolved from a utilitarian item designed to keep people in the harsh winters warm, to, as Védís Jónsdóttir said, "like a flag."

Þorgrímur reflects on the evolution of the lopi with obvious pride and shares the concerns of many Icelanders. "They've matured into a very fashionable item, and they're very expensive. What is sad about it is that the tourism industry skyrocketed in Iceland a couple of years ago. After the crash in 2008 and the value of our currency was really attractive to tourism, they started to import sweaters made with machines in China, and they were not cheap. Since I get these as presents from my mom, I cannot tell you how much a hand-knitted Icelandic sweater costs in Iceland—I don't know. I would guess it would be hundreds of dollars, because it's one man or woman knitting, so it would be really expensive. But I heard from people they were really disappointed to see Chinese color-band being sold in tourist shops, and they were not cheap."

How long has he been a fisherman? I want to know.

"I started working on the trawlers in the late eighties," he says, "on square net vessels and ice-fish trawlers and freezing vessels. I ended up working all over the world: in Iceland, in Greenland, in America, the Middle East, and Africa."

"What's life like on a ship?" I ask, and for this he has no answer. The depths of my ignorance have very obviously been laid bare here. Everything I know about fishing comes from watching *Jaws*.

"I don't know what to tell you," he says after a pause. "We just fish."

I explain that I know nothing about fishing, but Þorgrímur has already gleaned this and looks in vain for a place to begin, as a physicist might take a long pause to ponder where to begin explaining lattice field theory to a cat.

"How long do you go out?" I ask, throwing both of us a lifeline.

"OK," he says, looking relieved to have a place to start shoveling knowledge into my empty head. "In Iceland it will be a thirty-day trip on a fishing vessel. Thirty days on and then you unload, so you work twelve hours a day for thirty days in a row. There are different types of fishing boats, which might affect things. A freezing vessel freezes everything at sea: fillets, headed, whole, everything. Usually a month at sea. Ice trawler cools the catch, which has been blooded and gutted, with ice and brings it ashore to be processed. COVID had a lot of influence on how long the boats are out. My last two trips, I was stuck on a ship because of COVID; those trips were two hundred seventy days." I make a horrified face, and he goes on, "The last trip was one hundred days, and the one before that was one hundred seventy-two days. That's not really healthy for a family man or for anyone in the family."

And it's not just fishing boats. In March 2020, ports started to close because of fear of the spread of COVID, not just by people on shore but by people on ships too. That year, the aircraft carrier USS *Dwight D. Eisenhower* and its tender ship, the USS *San Jacinto*, set a record for the longest number of consecutive days at sea for a military surface vessel, 161—a record that was broken that same year by the guided missile destroyer USS *Stout*, which avoided port for 208 days.

Looking up the hill, we can see Alon and Arwin packing the last bits of their tent into the RV, so we say goodbye and head back. On the way, I text Rebekka and ask about her designs and if she thinks they reflect a change in the way lopis were worn. "I do think zippers were a game changer for being able to cool off," she replies and then adds, "I didn't pioneer zippers on lopapeysas, but I happily adopted it. Buttoned sweaters had been a thing for a long time. Usually had these intricately scrolled metal buttons, which I hate because I have an aversion to all metal ornamentation on clothing."

Adventure: Jökulsárlón Glacier Lagoon

I must admit that a week ago "glacier" was a really vague concept in my head. I knew they were made of ice, but when people talked about "glaciers receding" and "glacial deposits," I usually just nodded and pretended that I understood. But now, having seen them up close, my head is packed with knowledge. Glaciers are fields of packed, unmelted snowfall on and between mountains that can pile up for tens of thousands of years. Not only does it keep compacting, but that snow all moves—very slowly. How slowly? It moves at a glacial pace. It creeps down the mountain, it pushes stuff with it, and it picks things up. And when the unstoppable, albeit very slow, glacier meets a five-ton rock, that glacier will just push that boulder along. Then when that glacier finally melts, you have a giant rock where no giant rocks should be. There are a number of places where glaciers end in the ocean; one of these is Jökulsárlón Glacier Lagoon, where the glacier is pushed right up to the water, and bits of it break off and float away. These broken-off pieces of glaciers floating around are icebergs. And in a few places across Iceland, you can actually see icebergs bobbing around and heading out to sea. Jökulsárlón is near Vatnajökull National Park, and it's a great place to see icebergs up close. You can get a boat tour from here, where they'll ride you right up to them, or you can hang around on the beach, where bits of them will wash up and you can pick them up. We pull up and are greeted by a large parking lot, a hot dog stand, and a smattering of tourists. Most of the tourists are hanging close to the parking lot, so walking for three minutes along the beach brings us to a pretty isolated area where we can look at the icebergs undisturbed by others. It's an incredible view. Some of the ice is a deep blue. One thing that's impressive is just how quickly the icebergs are zipping along in the lagoon, and in all sorts of directions, occasionally smacking into one another with terrific force, making a lot of noise. Some of the icebergs make it across the lagoon, almost out to sea, only to come hurtling back.

Icebergs at the Jökulsárlón Glacier Lagoon making their way into the sea.

Adventure: Skaftafell

We camp at Skaftafell, in the shadow of Hvannadalshnúkur, Iceland's highest peak. At 6,900 feet (2,110 m), it is the northwestern rim of the Öræfajökull volcano, and for about $500 you can get a guide to take you on the 15-hour trek to the top. We have no such lofty goals, but we do take an easy walk along a three-mile (five-kilometer) path to the foot of the glacier. It looks at first like we'll be able to get right up under it, but about 400 yards (365 m) out, a roaring spiderweb of wide streams cuts us off, glacier meltwater headed toward the ocean. So we stand and watch the water and look out into the bay, where icebergs mill about, and then we head back to the campsite. It's late, or at least I think it's late; it's hard to tell, since it's cloudy and the sun never sets. The campground is enormous and broken up into places for RVs and tents. There's a well-maintained restroom cabin with showers inside and a row of sinks outside. These are periodically visited by

people doing dishes or brushing their teeth. There are myriad trails headed out from the campground to waterfalls, to glacier hikes, to adventure.

The next morning, we wander over to the very well-equipped café, use their free Wi-Fi, and have some coffee, which continues to confuse me. I keep ordering "American" coffee, thinking it's what I'm used to, but it's never what I'm expecting. American coffee, as served in Iceland, is something like what I expect cowboys in the Old West might boil in an empty tin can that had recently held baked beans. It's a deep black, powerful, bitter, soupy mixture that gets aggressively in your face and wants to fight, rather than the meek, milky coffee that pours endlessly from Dunkin' boxes in meetings across the States. There is a plethora of cups of various sizes, and it all seems very confusing. The cheerful woman at the register points out the summit of Hvannadalshnúkur. "You can see it today," she says. "It's the highest point

Alon's view down into the valley really shows the glacier. Panoramic photo by Alon Abramson.

View from the café at Skaftafell: Hvannadalshnúkur in the background. Photo by Trillian Stars.

Thwarted by glacial meltwater. That's the foot of the glacier in the background, pushing icebergs out to sea. Trillian wearing a thrift store lopi.

in Iceland." And like many places we've been to, it makes me think what a remarkable view this is to have from your cash register every day, all day, just the vast expanse of planet Earth, majestic and monumental, just there for you to stare at.

While we're at the café, Alon has gotten up ambitiously early (I can't say "at dawn," because there's no dawn) to go for a 10-mile trail run that takes him high above the Skaftafellsjökull (it's technically redundant to say "Skaftafellsjökull glacier" because *jökull* means "glacier "in Icelandic). Looking at his photos later, it's easier to see how everything fits together. Skaftafellsjökull is about 6 miles (10 k) long and 1.75 miles (2 k) wide. It runs down this valley and dumps icebergs into the lagoon at the bottom, when it runs out of space. Were the ocean not there, the glacier would just keep pushing everything in front of it across dry land until the thaw. You can easily imagine the ice flowing down this valley (and it does: there's a scientific station about halfway up that takes stop-motion videos) and see the icebergs launching out to a new life at sea. From the visitors' center, you can book tours to walk on the glacier.

We get back in the RV and continue west; we're more than halfway through our journey. For much of the next 135 miles (217 k), we'll be driving along the coast with the North Atlantic out our windows and an incredible wind buffeting us. In travel writer Rick Steve's *10 Ways Iceland Can Kill You*, "wind" is listed as number one.

Trillian in the Everywhere Sweater and Learn to Chart Headband and Joan wearing the Lakeside Lopapeysa and a Learn to Chart Headband, enjoying the black sand beach.

Adventure: Black Sand Beaches

All beaches in Iceland have black sand, because all the rocks in Iceland are basalt. Over the years, the lava is crushed to sand. You can watch this in action at many of the beaches on the south coast, where the sand is dotted with smooth stones of varying sizes, each being slowly ground to powder by the waves. At one of the black sand beaches, we stop and walk out about 0.8 miles (1 k) to the sea. The sand is more like a soft powder than the beach sand we're all used to. There are shells and rocks—some jagged, some incredibly smooth—and a lost fishing net.[1] When we get to the water, I can't resist taking off my shoes and socks and wading into the North Atlantic. It's cold but not uncomfortable—actually a lot warmer than I'd expected it to be. The beaches along the south coast are extremely windy, and if you have any amount of hair, a headband is very helpful to keep it out of your eyes.

Back in the RV, I've been doing decreases on my lopi, and my stitches are getting very stretched out on the needles. I wander back to where Joan's sitting in her nest of yarn and pillows and tell her I think I've done all I can until I can find a pair of 16-inch (40-cm) circular needles.

"I always do this," she says, reaching between two of my stitches with one finger and pulling about 15 inches of cable through so that it just hangs in the air and all my stitches tighten together again. I stare at her solution with my eyes bugged out.

"You don't ever really need sixteen-inch circulars," she says. "Now keep on going." She goes back to knitting.

I feel like Luke Skywalker after he could almost see the remote.

1. Lost fishing nets that drift around the ocean catching and killing marine life are a huge problem. Iceland is now a member of GGGI, the Global Ghost Gear Initiative, which seeks to reduce or eliminate the amount of lost fishing gear wreaking havoc in the ocean. The GGGI trains people to recover lost gear and holds educational programs that teach fishers best environmental practices and how to recycle gear.

Vik

Vík í Mýrdal is a small town of about 300 people on the southern coast. But it's also one of the most visited towns in Iceland, partly because it's so close to Reykjavik, about two and a half hours if you don't stop. Although not many people live here, there's a deep tourist industry: depending on how you count things, there are somewhere between 10 and 30 hotels in Vik. It's also a really popular movie filming location (possibly because it's so close to Reykjavik and it has so many hotels). The opening scenes of *Rogue One* were filmed here, as well as the "Eastwatch by the Sea" episodes of *Game of Thrones* in seasons 5 and 6. The Icelandic Netflix series *Katla* is set here.[1]

Using Vik as your base of operations, you can climb on a glacier, ride a horse, explore an ice cave, visit a brewery, or just chill out on the beach. The campground is quiet, and the common area is nice, with electricity and tables and a friendly local who overhears us talking about puffins and says, "You can indeed see puffins. They live on that cliff, way down there." Puffins had been on our vague list of things to see, especially since Joan knitted a pair of lopis with puffins on them, but we'd kind of written them off as too difficult to get to. "I don't really understand the puffin thing," Kiddi had said back in Reykjavik. "I don't think any Icelanders really think of them as *Icelandic*; they're on some islands, and you have to take a boat to get to them." And this is true on all its faces—people not from Iceland always think of puffins when they think of Iceland, and they are a pain in the ass to get to see, especially up close. And while Iceland is the quasi-home to some six million puffins, they don't spend the whole year here. Most of their time is spent at sea. They come back in the summer to nest and lay eggs and do puffin things.

Puffins were lower on my list, since I packed photo gear for sweaters and not bird-watching. To get that classic close-up of a puffin with a beak full of sand eels, you need a giant lens that weighs more than most everything I brought with me, or you need to go all the way out to the West Fjords, but I was certainly up for walking down to the cliff and having a look. The town is empty and covered in fog, and there's nobody on the beach. It's a long

So tantalizingly close to done is this lopi! Joan wearing the Lakeside Lopapeysa. Photograph by Trillian Stars.

---

1. Before any of that, though, it was here that Sólstafir shot the video for "Miðaftann," from their 2015 album *Ótta*, where a guy in a black lopi sweater washes up on the beach and wanders into a cave.

Photographing at the beach at Vik. Joan is wearing the Adventure Sweater. Kyle's wearing a Hot Springs Hat. Photo by Trillian Stars.

walk along crashing, thunderous waves through the black sand and occasional patches of incredibly smooth stones, and as we get closer to the cliffs, there are birds everywhere—flying around us, going in and out to sea—and on a high rock formation, two dozen heads peer down at us: puffins. They look at us, they look out to sea; they don't seem particularly bothered or interested. Periodically one leaps into the air and flies with incredible speed out to the ocean. I can't tell if they're returning with beaks filled with food, because they're so fast and relatively far away. But for a magical time, we're surrounded by hundreds of them.

The next afternoon we visit Smiðjan Brugghús, one of the local breweries that opened in 2018. There's typical bar food, a range of beer, and a big window looking into the brewing apparatus. Beer is a relatively new addition to Iceland, but you wouldn't know it by how much of it there

seems to be now. In 1915, the population voted, overwhelmingly, to ban beer. This prohibition continued in various forms for 75 years (eventually very low-strength beer was allowed, but at 2.25% it wouldn't excite most Americans). The ban was finally lifted in 1989, and Icelanders have hit the ground running with a whole bunch of local craft brews, including pilsners, lagers, stouts; pale, white, red, and Scotch ales; as well as IPAs and wheat beers that will keep any beer lover happy. (The price, however, is a different story.)

Alon's happy to sit in a brewery on a day when he doesn't have to drive and can relax. Afterward we wander down to the beach and photograph some sweaters. The sun pops out for a few minutes, and things look cheerful.

My lopapeysa is almost done. I've finished most of the yoke, and all that remains are ten or fifteen rows.

Knitter Profiles:
Anna Halla, Hera, and Guðlaug

"Welcome to the moon," says Hera Hjartardóttir, waving her arm out the window of her car at the lava fields. And in fact, that's not a great stretch of the imagination. In 1967, in what NASA referred to as a *planetary analogue campaign*, the Apollo 11 astronauts—Neil Armstrong, Buzz Aldren, and 30 of their colleagues—did use this area, Eldhraun, to practice for their time on the earth's largest satellite two years later. The undulating basalt fields closely mimic the rocky surface of the moon—although Eldhraun, unlike the moon, is also covered in a thick and delicate moss, turning everything green as far as the eye can see (except when it snows; then everything turns white).

In 1783, the volcano Lakagígar erupted for nearly a year, spewing lava and ash, killing half of the domestic animals on Iceland and nearly a quarter of the population. Many of those who survived fled to Denmark during a time known as

Móðuharðindin—the "hardships of the mist" (and why this is not the name of an Icelandic heavy metal band, someone will have to explain to me). Today Eldhraun is a field of rock 12 feet (3.7 m) thick, covering more than 500 square miles (800 km) on the western coast of Iceland. It's the main landscape of nearly anywhere you go.

Hera was born in Iceland but has spent her life going back and forth between here and New Zealand, singing pop-ish folk songs in both Icelandic and English. While talking, she slips effortlessly between the two languages. Today she's picked us up to show us around her country.

Like all the Icelanders we've met, she's enamored of this place—its geology, geography, and history—and it seems to give her a sense of strength and belonging. Also like many of the Icelanders we've met, she's wearing a lopapeysa sweater, with its patterned yoke and earth tones from undyed

At left is Dr. Ted Foss, a geologist, wearing the lopapeysa and leading a group of NASA astronauts on a training mission in the Askja crater in July 1967. Apollo 15 astronaut Al Wordon said of the experience, "I felt as if I were already on the moon." (NASA Image)

wool—the distinctive uniform of both rural and urban Iceland.

I mention to Hera what Mikael has said about every Icelander having three lopapeysas, and she confirms that it's mostly true. Once again, I'm racking my brain trying to think of something comparable for Americans, but the United States has no object that ties you so fully to your family and to your country.

At the moment, her album *Hera*, her tenth, is the number-one album in Iceland, beating out foreigners Taylor Swift and Billie Eilish. "I'm at a bit of a loss for words," she says, but seems to be taking it in stride. She's had a long career in Iceland, previously having been named the Best Female Artist at the Icelandic Music Awards (beating out local favorite Bjork, who'd won it six years running previously) and scoring at least one gold album. A lot of Hera's music, at times bouncy, pop, acoustic guitar–driven, and at other times sweeping and somber, is about home and comfort, so it's not unexpected that she's also a prodigious knitter and has a lot to say about it.

Hera's taking us to Reykjadalur, the Valley of Smoke, to meet her frænka Guðlaug (a.k.a. Gulla), who's been making lopapeysas her entire life. We travel through a lava field, climb over some small mountains and down into a valley, and, sure enough, the landscape is dotted with geothermal activity. In America, you'd think it was a series of brush fires. Gulla's house is off to the side of a quiet suburban street with large lawns. Through her open garage door, we spy boxes and boxes and boxes of yarn stacked and sorted by color. Joan's eyes get big.

We find Gulla in her immaculate garden, tending to the flowers. She's more than happy to talk about lopapeysas.

"The first one I made was for my doll," she says, leading us through the back door and producing a black-and-white photo from a shelf of a small girl holding an even smaller doll. "I was probably four when I knitted it."

"She built her house herself, using wood from banana crates," Hera tells us. And Gulla is very proud of her house, which she's upgraded over the years and which gives no clue that it was once made from cast-off packaging materials. She tells us that when she had the opportunity, she raised the roof 30 inches. It also has an immaculate French garden and a greenhouse that stays warm in the winter—filled with chairs so that people can visit, surrounded by warmth and flowers during the cold months.

She gives us a tour. "My house has no doors on the inside, and no stairs, and it has no bedroom. I built it for myself." Indeed, it has no bedroom and, barring the two bathrooms, every room opens up onto every other. Gulla doesn't believe in single-purpose areas. She has a bed in the kitchen and another on the sunporch, nearby everything that she needs. The house is filled with books and tapestries that she's woven and rocks she collected with her late husband. "We would pack a rucksack and head into the mountains for two weeks at a time." The constant motion of the backpack up and down over the years felted the back of her lopi sweater. She has three (just like Mikael said): one she knitted in the 1950s, in blue; a cardigan, the one she mainly wears now; and her late husband's, which she'll wear over her own if it's particularly cold out. ("He was a pretty large fellow," she says, donning his sweater to demonstrate.)

After we settle down in the French garden, admiring the flowers, Gulla's daughter Anna Halla arrives. Her backyard butts up against her mother's, and they spend the days going back and forth between one another's homes. When Anna Halla hears that we're talking about lopapeysas, she disappears for a moment and returns with a stack of magazines and scrapbooks: the patterns that they've shared for the past 50 or so years. Some go all the way to back to the 1950s and look much different, more angular, than the designs today.

"Where did you get your patterns before this?" I ask, pointing at a magazine.

"They were in our heads," Gulla replies.

In the 1950s, the women knitted together, and the men knitted too—though Guðlaug tells us her husband was more of a *functional* knitter than an aesthetic one. They all laugh remembering a hat that he repaired with cable instead of yarn and that had unruly bits sticking out of the top, although everyone admits that it functioned just fine as a hat. Gulla's father, Björn (Hera's great-grandfather), had a penchant for crocheting welcome mats out of spare fishing line. At the time, everybody worked in the fishing industry. Gulla made nets for catching herring and cod and found the handwork to be very similar to knitting. She was fast and made more money than a lot of other people. But then the herring went away.

Anna Halla tells us how they used to knit mittens with two thumbs so that when one thumb wore out you could just push it back inside the glove and push the other thumb out and not lose any time having to darn something. Knitting was functional,

Anna Halla, Hera, and Guðlaug in sweaters Anna and Guðlaug have made over the years. The sweaters Anna Halla and Hera are wearing were both knit in the 1960s.

though there was no reason that it shouldn't be beautiful as well. She says that she's been going through yarn that's been in their house for decades, trying to use it all up before buying more, and inside many of the balls of yarn, she'll find a note from her father with a message like "This ball of yarn was wound on December 9, 1961," and a few words about what's been going on. It inspires her to keep knitting.

Gulla shows us a lopi sweater that she knitted in the 1960s. It's seen almost daily use for decades and still looks new. There is a joy they're expressing in pulling things out of the closet to show us.

"You're not a person until you have a lopapeysa," says Anna Halla.

"Oh, come now," says Hera, "of course you are!"

"The lopapeysa *is* Iceland. Having one means that you're one of us."

Despite Hera's protestations, there seems to be some truth to this. "Lopapeysas are usually gifts," she tells us later when we're back in the car. "You can't really buy one for yourself. But I have a friend who didn't have a mother or a grandmother who knit, so he had no lopapeysa, and in Iceland you can't ask for a sweater, someone has to give it to you—so I knitted one for him."

I'm left again to wonder how a national identity can be so closely tied to something that people often behave so indifferently about. I think of Addi

Gulla shares the contents of a trunk filled with Iceland's fiber history.

telling us it's just a sweater but then wearing it onstage, and of the fisherman at Kleifarvatn telling us he didn't really think about his grandmother while still wearing the sweater he'd appropriated from his brother after she made it 20 years ago. But then, at the same time, Anna Halla, Hera, and Gulla positively beam when talking about them. I still can't wrap my head around it.

Gulla pulls out her family knitting gear and shows it to Hera and the rest of us. From her mother's knitted slippers, to devices for carding and spinning, Gulla has a trunk filled with Iceland's fiber history going back more than a century.

One tantalizing clue that Hera finds in the mix of patterns and books and balls of yarn is a photo from the 1930s of an extremely lopi-like sweater that turns out to be from a Norwegian pattern designer named Annichen Sibbern Bøhn, who was inspired by a 1930 Danish/Norwegian film called *Eskimo*, in which Swedish actress Mona Mårtenson plays an Inuit Greenlander named Eukaluk who spends a lot of time plucking her eyebrows, saving marooned sailors, and wearing opulent Greenlandic costumes with patterned yokes. After seeing the movie (which was exhaustingly filmed four times by the same cast to create a silent version as well as something new, three "talkies" in Danish, German, and French—*Eskimo* was the first Danish talking picture), Annichen Bøhn whipped up a pattern that she called "Eskimo" and published it in the Norwegian women's magazine *Urd* and then again in her book, *Knitting Patterns*, where it became wildly popular, as did talking films.

A model, possibly Annichen Sibbern Bøhn herself, wearing the sweater Eskimo sometime after 1930.

Annichen Sibbern Bøhn's Eskimo pattern.

I'm unable to find the movie, but a lot of poking around in an entire warren of rabbit holes leads me to the Danish Film Institute, which has a bunch of stills in their archive, and I see that Mårtenson's costumes do have an extremely lopi-like appearance, though they seem to be made of beads and worn as a capelet.

The photo that Hera has found turns out to be possibly even Annichen Sibbern Bøhn herself modeling the Eskimo pattern sweater sometime around 1930. All this would have been missed had it not been for a Danish scholar named Astrid Oxaal, who was flipping through a copy of *Urd* magazine 48 from 1930 and spotted something that she thought looked very lopi-like.

In 2003, Oxaal wrote a paper about her discovery in the Norwegian journal *Kunst og kultur* (arts and culture) called "Et norsk strikkemønster fra Grønland"—"A Norwegian sweater from Greenland."

Mona Mårtenson, the Inuit Greenlander Eukaluk, from Eskimo, *1930.*

After much stumbling around a maze of academic web pages in Norwegian (and discovering that the Norwegian word for "pattern" is "mønster"), I manage to buy a copy of "Et norsk strikkemønster fra Grønland" for 149 Norwegian kroner (which turns out to be about $17), but it maddeningly arrives without any illustrations—just captions. But Oxaal had tracked down Bøhn's daughter, Sidsel, in January 2003 and got some firsthand information from her about the history of Eskimo, including that it was made out of pretty traditional colors—white, black, and brown—instead of the bright colors of the movie capelet.

Annichen Sibbern Bøhn seems to have been very much like Auður Laxness in that she championed the domestic handicrafts of her country and wrote about them extensively in popular magazines. It seems difficult to believe that Laxness, writing as she did for so many magazines, traveling a lot, and making an effort to stay abreast of international fashion, would have been unaware of Bøhn's extremely popular

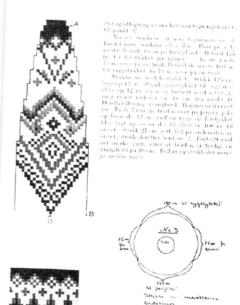

Possibly the proto-lopi? Designed by Annichen Sibbern Bøhn and published in Urd *magazine in 1930.*

A cornucopia of wool, magazines, and knitting tools at Hannyrðabúðin, in Selfoss.

sweater. And while Eskimo is definitely lopi-like, it is also decidedly *not* lopi-like in some ways. I find it extremely believable that Auður Laxness could have seen this sweater and the colorful designs of South America and the *Icelandic Sjónabók* and merged all of these in her head to produce a truly, uniquely Icelandic variant based on a multitude of influences.

Now Hera takes us to Hannyrðabúðin, a handicraft store that her frænkas have owned for 50 years. It's only about 20 minutes away. Inside are collections of knitting patterns going back decades, including bright neon lopi designs from the 1980s, with each generation making their own modifications to knit in who they are.

Co-owners Þóra and Alda are both working today and show us how the wool, unspun, is gathered into plates and how easily it can be pulled apart and how you would pull one end from the top and another from the bottom and hold the two together in two strands as you knit, as we'd seen in Mývatn. The store has original undyed wool, representing the natural colors of the sheep, but also a variety of reds and blues and greens for more modern patterns.

From there, we visit three other nearby wool stores, one attached to a sheep farm, which has only lopapeysa sweaters, wool, and yarn, all within a few miles. Then we get back in the car, and Hera drops us off back at the RV.

Knitter Profile:
Janina Witzel

My sweater, so close to finished, seems to taunt me. And I decide to just wear it with the needles still in it; it's 95 percent of a lopapeysa—I figure, that's enough to wear around town.

We meet knitter Janina in the southern coastal town of Hveragerði. Depending on who you ask, Hveragerði is either called "Earthquake Town" or "Hot Spring Town" because of all the geothermal activity. Hveragerði is home to about 2,500 people, making it one of the larger places that we've visited. At the very pink Orkan gas station on Breiðamörk, a French tourist who's been waiting here a week for friends to get out of jail in Paris tells me, while spraying a mouthful of sunflower seeds in a continuous, sputtering stream that never seems to need refilling, that the ground is so hot here you can cook food by just burying it for a

couple of hours. He swears that he's been cooking fish that way for a week. I listen in half-attentive fascination while watching the RV consume an alarming amount of gasoline.

Janina is from Germany originally, came to Iceland first as an au pair eight years ago, and ended up staying. Now she teaches school, raises Norwegian Forest cats, and knits lopapeysas. "Sometimes I knit with friends," she tells us, "but mostly by myself." Her own sweaters have bold colors and a distinctive rolled edge above the ribbed collar made by five knit rows of a different color. "I just like the way that looks," she says. Over the years she's come up with body and arm styles that she likes, and she assembles those parts into wonderful creations for her friends and family.

Machine-made, lopi-inspired knitwear is available at pretty much every gas station and convenience store around the Ring Road.

Back in Hestaland, everybody was wearing a lopi that their German au pair had knitted for them, so I ask Janina if there's some connection between lopis and au pairs from Germany.

"I certainly knew about these sweaters before I came here," she says. "I knew about them in Germany, but I had no idea how to make them. And I had some friends visit while I was here who convinced me to start knitting. But I think a lot of au pairs start knitting because the mom they're with knits and shows them—or someone else in the family. Knitting is such an Icelandic thing, and you have so much free time as an au pair that I think people just start doing it. And being in Iceland, you have to knit a lopi. It's also something that you can take with you wherever you go."

And, in fact, it turns out that years after she arrived, Janina herself hired an au pair who took up knitting while she was in Iceland, so it comes full circle.

We talk for a while at her long, wooden dining room table, enjoying coffee that I find appropriately familiar while we are all vying to provide the most enticing-looking lap to two enormous cats that wander through the room and pay us scant attention before climbing into an enormous cat tree and staring languorously out the window into the drizzle.

Janina isn't sure you can cook by burying food, though her backyard is filled with thriving plants and yellow flowers, watched over by a large, open-air enclosure that the cats can venture safely into. I put my hand on the ground, and it's damp and cold.

The residents of Hveragerði have harnessed the readily available geothermal warmth to become Northern Europe's largest producer of bananas, with a small plantation at Garðyrkjuskóli Ríkisins, a.k.a. the Icelandic Agricultural University, which has been growing the South American fruit since

Page from the Icelandic Sjónabók of Jón Einarsson, Sjónabók frá Skaftafelli, *published in 1994 by Má l og menning. Photograph by Gudmundur Ingolfsso.*

Janina in the Vik Dress. The winds along the south coast are notorious.

the 1950s, along with coffee beans and avocados. This has become more important since the early 2000s, when Iceland decided it wanted to become carbon-neutral and to try growing foods that were traditionally imported. Icelanders import nearly five tons of bananas each year (some of which are in our RV). Ultimately, the university is only able to produce a ton of bananas each year, but as proof of concept, it's possible.[1]

It's also here that I see, for the first time, a copy of the *Icelandic Sjónabók*, which, it turns out, is a name given to a collection of ten manuscripts by a group of different authors compiled in the 17th, 18th, and 19th centuries. The one I get to see (or rather, the reproduction of it; the original is in the museum in Reykjavik) was compiled by a farmer from Skaftafell named Jón Einarsson who lived

between about 1731 and 1798, and consists of 49 pages that have patterns on one side printed out on hand-drawn graph paper. Lots of these designs feature the eight-petaled rose, and look like they're made for needlepoint. But here it is—the very early language of Icelandic design.

We venture outside, where the wind is blowing fiercely in from the coast, and the rain starts pelting us. Janina's umbrella inverts itself in seconds, and we decide that we're just going to get wet.

Wind and waves along the south coast can be extremely dangerous. They cause frequent close calls and occasional deaths. In 2017, a German tourist got pulled out to sea; so did a man from China in 2016 and an American in 2007.

As for adventures, Janina suggests the coast, but there's also . . . the hot river.

---

1. https://grapevine.is/mag/articles/2013/12/02/the-mythical-banana-kingdom-of-iceland.

Adventure: The Hot River

The hot river is a geothermally heated natural stream in Reykjadalur Valley, accessible after an arduous three-mile (five-kilometer) hike over some substantial hills with spectacular views. At the beginning of the trail is a parking lot and a café (remember this, it will be useful later). Along the way to the geothermal area, you will see sheep and wildflowers, fumaroles and waterfalls. The trail is well marked and well maintained, but be prepared to go over or through some small streams and do a lot of uphill walking. The first big hill we walk up takes us right inside a cloud, and visibility plummets. In the distance, shapes that may be other hikers appear and disappear. Occasionally a dripping wet person propped up by two hiking poles staggers down past us, and I try to judge the look on their face: Is it happiness? Is it terror? Regret?

When you think you must surely have walked three miles quite some time ago, you'll see a sign promising that the thermal river is just 700 meters (2,300 feet) ahead. After what feels like another five kilometers, the river (stream—really, it's a stream) acquires a boardwalk alongside of it and some low walls that you may (or may not) be able to hide behind to change modestly. The river is superheated by geothermal activity close to the surface, and, in fact, all around the valley are pools of water and mud that are literally boiling—these are usually marked with signs announcing that you will be killed by Iceland if you try bathing there.

Despite the damp and cold, there are more people than we expect at the destination. Perhaps 20 people are spread out along 50 yards (55 m) of stream. In some places, the boardwalk descends to the water to make getting in and out easier. The stream is hotter the farther up you go and is cooled by meeting another stream of ordinary, ice-cold mountain water. Above the mixing place, the water is very hot, like a bath that's a couple of degrees above where it ought to be. Twenty yards (18 m) farther downstream, it's comfortably warm, so comfortably warm you may want to stay there all day.

The weather starts to worsen pretty much immediately after we get in the water. Everything was already soaked, but now the rain has picked up and the wind has become substantial. The river is so warm and comfortable that the thought of

At the hot river: Arwin leading the way, Joan in the Adventure Sweater, and Alon and Trillian in Hot Springs Hats.

Not getting out. Joan wearing the Learn to Chart Whale Headband.

getting out of it into the 40 degree F (5 C) air and stinging wind seems ever more and more dreary. So we sit, feeling content but apprehensive as we watch our pile of clothes become slowly, completely, and thoroughly soaked. There is absolutely no way we are going down this mountain dry, and that thought weighs heavily on me. So many of Iceland's joys seem to come from first making yourself incredibly uncomfortable and then stopping the thing that feels so awful.

Eventually we realize that despite all our hopes and wishes, the weather is only going to get worse. So we climb, yelping and shrieking, out of the perfectly warm water into the frigid air and start putting on our wet clothes. My lopi at least is dry, as I'd put it under my waterproof jacket, but my pants are as soaked as though I'd worn them into the river. Water comes out the sides of my shoes when I pick them up. I put on a damp shirt, my lopi, and my waterproof layer, throw the backpack on, and we head out, squishing. The wind has picked up to 50 mph (80 kph), which is enough to blow an uncautious trekker from the trail into the ravine below. I keep that in mind, but I also keep my eyes riveted to the step in front of me; lifting your head brings the pain of sharp, stinging rain into your eyes. However wet and miserable most parts of me are, the lopi is keeping my trunk warm, and the waterproof layer is keeping at least half of me from getting wetter. The hike up the mountain seemed long; the hike back, besides being largely downhill, seems to take so much longer.

But after an uncomfortable, interminable walk, we round a hill and can see, far away in the valley below, the café and the parking lot. It's still very far away, but being able to see it makes the journey seem less arduous.

We stagger into the café, where a number of tourists between the ages of "retired long ago" and "college student" have simply stripped off their pants and shirts and are ordering hot chocolate in their underwear as though it were the most normal thing. I sit down on a chair by an enormous window that shows the beautiful vista, made now more beautiful by the fact that it is no longer attempting to destroy me. The café has a variety of cakes, beverages, and sandwiches—and a fireplace. I set my shoes next to the fire, and some French cyclists do the same. One at a time, those in our group take turns going out to the RV and changing into drier clothes, throwing all the wet ones into grocery store bags. While I'm there, I notice that one of the needles has come unscrewed from my cable and is somewhere between here and the hot spring. This bothers me more than maybe it should—not just because I'm upset that I've littered, but also now that I may not be able to finish the sweater at all.

"How silly is that?" says Joan, back at the café, producing a spare set of needles from her knitting bag, which she inexplicably seems to have carried all the way to the hot river and back. "Let's just buy you a new set of needles next time we pass a wool store. They'll be your Iceland knitting needles, and they'll be something to remember."

This sounds like an excellent idea.

After an hour or so reflecting and enjoying not being soaked, we head to the campground, stay up well into the night talking about the day's adventures and laughing at what had been tragedy mere hours ago, and fall asleep swiftly.

Adventure: Nauthólsvík Geothermal Beach

The next day Hera calls and asks if we want to hang out again, which sounds like an excellent idea. Trillian and I agree—while Joan and the others go off in search of waterfalls.

Hera suggests Nauthólsvík Geothermal Beach, which isn't far from her house. After nearly freezing to death the day before, luxuriating in a hot tub sounds like a great idea, especially since the RV has become filthy—filled with gritty black mud and the smell of damp socks. Nobody wants to be there anymore. All the romance has left from our house on wheels. Nauthólsvík bills itself as Iceland's only white sand beach—which is really a bit misleading since the beach itself is actually made of black sand that's had hundreds of tons of white sand imported from Italy dumped on top of it. Nauthólsvík also has a seawall, which creates a lagoon into which geothermally heated water is dumped, all to give Icelanders some impression of what it must be like to go to the beach somewhere else in Europe. And at times, the beach is packed like the Riviera, with hundreds of Icelanders sitting out on the white sand on beach towels and wading out into the warm lagoon. Today's not like that, though. Maybe 50 people are here today. We plop ourselves down in one of the long pools, surrounded by old men who have been coming here to soak every day for years. Occasionally one of them gets up and heads slowly to the water outside the seawall for a slow swim in the 46 F (8 C) degree ocean before sauntering back to restart their heart in the lagoon. Despite the white sand gimmick, this may be my favorite of all the swimming pools we've visited. The hot tub is enormous. We spend some time talking about Hera's new album, the recording of which spanned three years, and the resulting tour and what it's like to be a musician in the 21st century. Occasionally someone walks past, does a double take and says "Hera?!?!" sings a line from her number-one album, then gushes in Icelandic about her music before bouncing off, making us feel a little special.

After an incredibly luxurious afternoon, Hera drops us back at the RV, and we start the

At the white sand beach.

There's nothing quite like knitting your own lopapeysa while you're in Iceland. Photos by Trillian Stars.

penultimate leg of our journey back to Reykjavik. While we drive, I finish up my lopi and try to put it on, only to discover that I bound off the collar too tightly and my head won't fit through it.

"Frog it back!" commands Joan, imitating a frog. "Ripit ripit ripit!"

With a grimace I cut the neck of my sweater and pull back about 15 rows, then dive into it again, threading Joan's spare needles through exposed loops and hoping I'm not twisting stitches. This time I add the rolled neck that I'd seen on Janina's sweaters, but I do it in orange after ten rows of brown—to represent the volcano—and instead of weaving the trailing end in, I stitch it down the neck of the sweater, like the lava we saw coming down the mountain. It feels fitting that this—the shapes, the meanings, the features—are all constructed things that I've seen on this trip, that it's a tapestry

of this month in Iceland, and I can look back at all the parts and know where they came from.

This time when I put my head into the sweater, it comes out the other side. VICTORY!

Suddenly all this seems to make more sense to me: Guðlaug and her friends trading patterns in their minds, Palla adding helicopters for her little frændi who loves helicopters, the *Icelandic Sjónabók*, the eight-petal rose, Auður Laxness and her book of South American art—all these things are part of the language of the lopapeysa, a language of which I can now speak a few faltering words. These are the things that are used to spell the story of these people in this time and place and that celebrate this strange burning and freezing island in the North Atlantic and that make them and it different from everywhere else.

Knitter Profile: Védís Jónsdóttir

The next day, Joan and I meet up with Védís Jónsdóttir, who's without a doubt the most important knitwear designer in Iceland at the moment. She's got her long chestnut hair in a half bun and is wearing a lopi called NEI, which means *no*. ("It's good to wear for protesting," she says.) On and off for the past 29 years, Védís has been the lead designer at *the* Icelandic yarn company Ístex, and the editor of *Lopi*, its annual look book and pattern collection. She's not sure how many sweaters she designs in an average year. "I have taken time off," she says. But this year? Looking up into the sky and counting in her head: "Thirty?" She's designed a lot of sweaters. She says she stopped counting long ago at 180, when she was designing ready-to-wear wool garments.

One thing we're very curious about is, what makes a lopi sweater? We've seen so many things, from very traditional to designs that pare things down to the shadow of a pattern and are almost daring to be called out as not-quite-a-lopi sweater.

"The most important part," she says, "is that it's made from lopi. That's what makes a lopapeysa a lopapeysa, and then of course it's the pattern and the form—the yoke has to fit what we call a traditional lopapeysa. In the older days, it had a mirroring border at the cuffs and at the waist. It's also important that it's hand-knitted and not machine-knitted.

"Of course, things develop and change, and designers will push the envelope. There has been a lot of debate lately that a lopapeysa can only be a lopapeysa if it's knitted by an Icelandic woman in Iceland. And this is true of something like Harris Tweed, which has to be woven on the island of Harris in the weaver's home. My sister lives in the US. She's Icelandic. She buys lopi, and she knits. Is it not a lopapeysa anymore because she's knitting it in the US? It's difficult. I don't like it when I see machine-knitted sweaters that are called lopapeysa. And if they are raglan, it's not a lopapeysa. It has to be knitted in the round with the decreases all around."

Védís has an infectious love for Icelandic handicrafts and has spent her entire life growing up with them. She seems less concerned with arguing details and more concerned with spreading the love of lopi and the tradition of Icelandic knitting.

"In the old days," she tells us, "everybody had to knit because we had so few resources. There was no money in the country. We had no way to import things. So people had to knit socks and sweaters. My grandmother started knitting lopapeysa, I think, for a hospital fundraiser. She'd knitted other things, of course, but I think that was her first lopapeysa. I remember she would knit on weekdays and do embroidery on Sundays. She had a collection of leaflet patterns, and she would sketch patterns; she would do very classic patterns." Védís doesn't even remember learning how to knit, it was just always there, and now from her vantage point of being Iceland's top professional knitwear designer, she probably knows more about modern lopi than anyone else in the world. I imagine that she must see things differently—that she must see wholly formed words and thoughts where the rest of us just see symbols.

"When you see someone wearing a lopapeysa," I ask, "what are the chances that you'll know the name of the pattern it's knitted from?"

"High," she laughs, and then laughs again. "Very high. Even higher if it's one that I designed." A grin stretches across her face. "I remember there was a big change in 2003 or 2004, when the lopapeysa became really popular again and it wasn't considered nerdy. I made a really slim, fitted one with a zipper, and we'd never put anything online and we thought, *Oh, this internet! Maybe we should try that!* So we put this pattern out, and it became immensely popular. I remember there was a culture night in Reykjavik, and I just stopped counting how many people I met wearing that sweater." She shakes her head like she's been shocked and laughs again. "It was very strange."[1]

"It's a little bit the same with Riddari," she continues, "which is the most popular sweater I designed for Ístex. If you look on Instagram, it's just everywhere—and someone told me that in Finland, there are more than three hundred thousand Riddari sweaters. In Finland. That's a lot. It's nice. Especially if I see them in nice colors!"

---

1 "This is the very sweater, Æði (which means 'frenzy'), that Sæþór was wearing in Seltún. The design is so popular in Iceland it's been featured on candles, napkins, matchbooks, and even livestock feed bags."

Janina in a Riddari sweater designed by Védís in 2008.

But how did she get here? What's the trajectory from sitting with your grandmother watching her knit on weekdays to the top of the fiber arts world? Well, it wasn't planned, that's for sure.

"I was always drawing when I was a kid," Védís says. "Always drawing ladies in elaborate clothes, and my grandfather said, 'Can't you draw something nice? Like a dog? Or a horse?' But I would draw ladies and glue paper together to make their hair pieces bigger.... I was not a farmer-to-be. ... I wanted to be a painter and study art, but at some point I thought, *I want to be a designer,* when I found out that *designer* is something that you could do.

"I had a summer job, when there was still a big wool industry in Iceland, designing ready-made garments. They liked my work, and when I graduated from the design school of the Royal Danish Academy in Denmark, I was offered a job

with Álafoss. And I thought, *Oh, I'm going back to Iceland.* Which I hadn't planned. So I started making ready-made garments. Although I had always knitted, I never thought, *I'll be a hand-knit designer,* but then when Álafoss went bankrupt, Ístex was founded by some of the workers, and they asked if I could come and be a consultant, so I started revitalizing old hand-knitting patterns. Guðríður Ásgeirsdóttir was doing the instructions, but I was doing the colorways, adapting the sizes, and modernizing the sweaters. I didn't find it very satisfying; it's *good* to adapt old patterns and make them better while trying to protect the integrity of the design, but it wasn't what I wanted to be doing, so I started designing hand-knits myself.

"Though that doesn't mean knitting. For a lot of my work, I only do swatches." She holds up her hands to indicate something the size of a washcloth. "Then I do the math that has to be right for the pattern, shape, and wool. I tell people *I knit in my head.* I don't knit sweaters. My daughter had friends come over from school and they're like *Oh! Are you knitting a sweater?* Nope. I'm doing a swatch. And my daughter told them all, 'She never knits anything that makes sense!' So I knit swatches; then I write the instructions in all sizes. I always have a pretty clear idea of how it will look, and obviously I couldn't do what I do if I was knitting all day. That's the biggest misunderstanding about my job.

"I learned design. I'm very respectful of other people's work and the elements of their designs—it's the same with music or books, you wouldn't copy a paragraph from someone's book. But design is a jungle. It's like there are no rules."

As for where the lopapeysa came from, Védís has yet to see convincing evidence of the Auður Laxness story.

"The woolen mills were making lengths of wool that would then be spun, but at some point, those two women from West Iceland decided to try knitting the unspun wool, and that's where I think the plötulopi developed from—and then the sweaters with contributions from many women. This story about Auður Laxness, I had never heard it until Ásdís Jóelsdóttir's book. I think there's pressure to come up with something new. The photo in the book shows Auður wearing a beautiful raglan sweater, and other people were making raglan sweaters like that at the time. Auður was artistic and a very good knitter and cared for Icelandic handicraft and culture; of that, there is no question. But that she designed the first lopapeysa?" Védís shrugs. "I remember I heard this story on the radio and thought, *What?! Auður Laxness invented the lopapeysa; how interesting.* And a friend called me and said, 'Did you hear that?' And I said, 'I heard it, but I've never heard it before.' Auður lived in Mosfellsbær, which is *very* close to Álafoss, and we thought it was very strange that nobody had ever mentioned it. Nobody at Ístex has any record that she ever designed for Álafoss. So . . . that was some news to me. I think people want it to be a famous person who's invented something instead of it being a thing that evolved by the work of not-famous people."

"What about the Annichen Sibbern Bøhn Eskimo pattern that we'd found at Gulla's?" I ask. And, of course, Védís has thought about this too.

"The Eskimo pattern is knitted from the neck down in much finer yarn," she says. "The yoke is seventy-one rounds, and the traditional lopapeysa was always knitted bottom up in three-ply plötulopi. And that's what is truly original about the lopapeysa—the stitches are bigger, so you need fewer rounds than with other patterns that were popular at the time. I think it comes from speed— that we didn't have much time to be sitting and knitting little stitches. You knit your Sunday best sweater out of a finer yarn. And Ásdís mentions in her book that when soldiers were in Iceland, they were looking for souvenirs to take home, and being able to knit them quickly would be an important part of a business.

"And from there, I think it got popular when they got easier to make. In 1967, Álafoss came out with

Álafosslopi, the thick one; that explains why the patterns all came out in the 1970s. You could knit from plötulopi, but you need a very soft hand or it breaks constantly, but when the Álafosslopi was made and exported, the lopapeysa became a *thing*, so it was quite recent. It's funny that people think the lopapeysa is an old thing and it's not. Even here in Iceland, when you go to a school play and the kids are saying, *Oh, here we are in ancient times in a turf house*, and they're wearing a lopapeysa—which I find very funny because it came much later. And it has become part of our national character now. I think what makes the lopapeysa so important to Icelanders is that it's something that everybody can have; it connects us. We saw it after the financial crisis that it became 'cool,' or right again, and it was the way to show that we are united instead of racing around in expensive cars and acting like we were rich. All of a sudden, all sorts of people who would not be wearing lopapeysas were wearing lopapeysas, and it has become like a flag. It was something everybody could wear and could afford. In my job people ask me, 'Don't you work with influencers?' And I say, 'Yes. Farmers and fishermen.' The popularity goes up and down; now it's up; of course, it will go down again. But it went from farmers and fishermen to everyone. If someone says they don't have one, everybody else will say, *What? You don't have a lopapeysa?!* I'm not a spokeswoman for consumption, but I think you should have many lopapeysas: one in bright colors, one in natural colors, one that's thick, one that's thin."

This sounds like a great plan.

Back Home

The next morning, we return the RV, which is a bit worse for wear. Even the well-maintained Ring Road is not always easy going, and you're reminded what a wild place Iceland is. Every year tourists die—swept out to sea, fallen from ledges, in plane crashes—and we've read that an average of six people a day are breaking an ankle at a volcano. Along the way we've lost a window, had a door vibrate out of its moorings, had drapes bounce down from the wall—and in the last 24 hours, the electricity ceased to function. For five people, it wasn't nearly as spacious as the photos would lead you to believe, and we're all very happy to stretch out again in Reykjavik, take long showers in unending hot water, wash our clothes, and lie about on furniture. It feels like we've had an adventure and have returned home. All the places in Reykjavik feel familiar. The bartender at Prikið asks how our trip was, and we say that it was long and amazing and that we're glad to be back and to stretch out.

We run into Kiddi at a café, and he tells us a story of Iceland's former president, Ólafur Ragnar Grímsson, going door to door in the town of Garðabær with a lost cat he'd found, trying to track down its people. It's a charming story and seems indicative of Iceland, a country where people have been shaped by the crucible of its extremes and have come to the conclusion that things are better if they try to help one another.

There's a banging on the window, and I look up to see Mikael waving in at us. He comes inside, and I'm feeling it's a bit like the last scene in *The Wizard of Oz*, where Dorothy's recuperating in bed and pointing at everyone saying, "And you were there! And you! And you!" Mikael states some vague plans in Icelandic that I don't quite understand, but he confers with Kiddi briefly before giving me a fist bump and heading out.

At Kattakaffihusid, the cat café, we meet Maria, who's an opera singer, classically trained pianist, and friend of Kiddi's. She's got blue-green hair, a tall, angular face, and a gigantic smile.

"How do you know Kiddi?" I ask.

"I posted on the internet that I needed a microphone stand, and he responded saying he had one that he didn't need." There's that Icelandic network doing what it does best.

It seems that everybody in Iceland is *doing something*. If they're not writing mystery novels or making records, they're singing opera or acting in movies. Iceland has the highest percentage of published authors on the planet. And for a country half the size of the city I live in, they have an incredible music and film scene. *How does this happen?* I wonder. Are people from Iceland so great, or are people in my city just particularly lazy?

Maria's wearing a very traditional brown and white lopi that Joan immediately asks her about.

"My ex's grandmother made it for herself. Probably in the 1970s or 1980s. The pattern is called Dalur. It means.... " She consults with Kiddi in Icelandic and then says, "The valley. It's from the old Icelandic word *dalr*. It's one of the very popular old patterns." I'm impressed that the patterns have names that people know and wonder about this hidden language. What does it say that you wear Dalur rather than some other pattern? Does it tell Icelandic knitters something about you? Do people wag their heads forlornly if you walk by in the wrong sweater pattern?

This word, *dalur,* is one we've come across before. The volcano Fagradalsfjall is three words—*fagur, dalur,* and *fjall*—which together mean "beautiful valley mountain"...though the dalur is quickly filling up with lava, so they might need to change the name if the eruption persists.

There are five cats in the Kattakaffihusid, but only two are interested in interacting with us. I can see one asleep in a felt pumpkin, occasionally opening one eye and deciding that there are too many people to be bothered coming out. I try to remember if it's the cappuccino or the latte that I've decided is the thing that's most like American coffee, and I order the wrong one yet again. This one arrives in a cup like a shot glass. I probably won't figure the coffee thing out until we're back home.

We learn that Kiddi's down to a single lopapeysa.

"I've always had two or three," he says, "but I'm down to one, which is why my mother made me that gray one that Guðný has. I've just always had them. In fact, I even had knitted underwear from my grandmother when I was a child."

This produces a giggle across the table.

Walking around Reykjavik with Maria in her sweater, Dalur, which was designed by lopapeysa titan Bára Þórarinsdóttir in 1970 and has remained very popular.

"Really itchy," he confirms. "It was extremely uncomfortable. I would put it on, just to please my grandmother, when I was maybe five or six. And she would always check," he laughs, remembering, "and then as soon as she was gone, my mom immediately had me take it off. I suppose my father had these too. But today you have cotton and stuff, which is much better. But!" he interrupts himself, lest we think he is not a fan of Icelandic knitting—he waves the sleeves of his lopi in the air—"for going out in almost any kind of weather, this is wonderful. They're comfortable."

Kiddi asks us about our trip, all the places that we've gone, and he nods approvingly while we talk. I mention that I'd wanted to go to Siglufjörður, which is where a bunch of novels I've been reading are set. Maria chimes in that the TV show *Trapped* was also set there. *Trapped* is another show we binge-watched a few months back. It's about a small-town police chief who gets divorced and has

to move in with his ex-wife's parents and solve a strange murder. We enjoyed it quite a bit. I ask Kiddi if he's seen it.

"Yes," he says, "I've seen that. There are really only a very few types of Icelandic TV shows; one is where a police officer from Reykjavik goes to someplace far away and then is shocked at how remote and provincial it is, and the difficult thing about that is the pretense that someone from Reykjavik is just going to Siglufjörður for the first time, when in reality everybody in Iceland has visited these places numerous times. The other type of show is where a woman is overwhelmed by her experiences in the city and moves to a farm, where she falls in love with a horse." Sniping at Icelandic television seems to be a national pastime for young people, who barrage the forums on Reddit after each episode, asking questions like, "Why did they take the samples to Vik? Why didn't they take them to Reykjavik? It's only an hour away." And "Where did that river come from? There's no river there. You can walk between those two places."

After the last cat decides she's had enough of people and jumps up on a transom eight feet in the air, we get up and take a walk through the center of town and then down to the harbor. It's good to be back after an adventure, and Reykjavik feels like a great place to just stop and sit and be for a while. Kiddi and the others have drifted ahead, and I notice that we're passing 12 Tónar, one of Reykjavik's several record stores. I run in and ask if they happen to have any Raggi Bjarna, the guy Eyþór had called the Icelandic Frank Sinatra. The clerk looks at me, unimpressed, and says, "Of course I have that," and hands me a four-CD boxed set without getting up. It's exactly as though I'd walked into a record store in Manhattan and asked, apologetically, if they'd ever heard of Frank Sinatra. I buy the CDs and put them in my backpack. 12 Tónar is not just a record store but a café and a bar and a concert venue, filled with soft chairs and places to relax. For 20 years, they've also produced local music, and the display tables are littered with up-and-coming new bands and samplers of Icelandic music. When I catch up to everyone else, I show my CDs to Kiddi and he is enthusiastically approving while looking at the selections on the back. "These are all very good," he says. Then, "Oh, hey, I didn't realize this; I play drums on this one right here."

Addi texts to ask when we're leaving. Sólstafir is playing a festival in the North, and he wants to know if we want to come along, but it's the day after we leave. I text back. "That's too bad," he says. Then ten minutes later, he texts again, "We're having a rehearsal tonight. We're going to go through the whole show really quick. Do you want to come to that?"

Of course we do.

That evening we head back to the rehearsal space and can hear drums from a block away. We walk inside, and the whole band is pressed together in a small space with the set list taped to a wall, cables and guitars and effects pedals everywhere. We stand in the doorway, and when the song they're playing ends, Addi, with no explanation to the rest of the band, says, "Hey, hello! Have a seat! There are seats, one behind that drum kit, one by the mixing board, and one in front of the amplifiers. We're going to try something here, since we're all using this magic technology of *in-ear monitors*"—he plugs some headphones into the jumble of cables and equipment and hands us

each a pair—"you should be able to hear everything now," he says, and they continue. Now we have vocals in one ear, guitars in another, drums and bass concussing our rib cages.

"This is our first concert since COVID!" says Addi after a song, and I realize he means us, here, in this rehearsal space, not the giant festival tomorrow. "It's nice to have you here." We watch them do the whole concert from three feet away, and then Addi drives us back to town while Joan asks more questions about sweaters. He waves when we get out of the car, and he drives off. Afterward someone says, "I wonder why they're so nice to us?" And I'm sure they were talking about Addi, but I'm also wondering why everybody we've met has been so nice to us. Presidents returning lost cats, college professors driving us to meet relatives.... I wonder how nice I'd be to an Icelander who called me out of the blue and said they were doing a book on baseball hats or something and could they photograph mine. I figure I'd probably be nice, but not this nice.

We stand around outside the Airbnb for a bit and decide that we're too pumped up from the concert to go back inside. I look up at the gray sky and wonder what time it may be and what anybody's doing. We walk downtown and sit at a café, where I text Eyþór to see what he's up to. He writes back a few minutes later that's he's gone to the Faroe Islands to set up a new branch of the scooter rental outfit and asks how long we'll be around. Sadly, not long. Later I realize I forgot to ask him to send photos of any sweaters he sees.

A few minutes later, Rä texts to say that Sæþór is done with rehearsal and they're going to go out, and are we doing anything? We're doing absolutely nothing. We meet them near our Airbnb and walk aimlessly across the city talking and snapping photos. Sæþór takes us to a park and a sculpture garden. I photograph Rä wearing our last sweater, which she loves, and Joan tells her to keep it. She hugs us both. Sæþór spends ten minutes trying to teach me how to say *Eyjafjallajökull*, the volcano that erupted in 2010 and shut down air travel across the Northern Hemisphere, but it's of no use. No matter how many times he says it, it always sounds like consonants are just falling from his mouth in a way they've never been connected before.

We have no destination and nothing that needs to be done, which is a wonderful feeling. I've been on edge for the whole trip with all the work hanging over us, worrying that there's some photo I forgot to get or didn't get properly.

Rä wearing the Hestaland Horse Sweater.

Eventually we end up at Dillon Whiskey Bar on Laugavegur, a small, loud bar that boasts 170 different types of whiskey and some of the drunkest people I've met in Iceland.

An old man in a flat cap and a tweed jacket comes up to us and stares silently at us from an uncomfortably close distance with a huge grin on his face.

"This is Arnleif," says Rä. "He's very famous, and he's very drunk." She shoos him away, "Go home, Arnleif; you're drunk; I love you." I sit next to Sæþór, and we talk about touring and guitars and songwriting and what's it's like to have been in a band for two decades. He's excited at the thought of playing out again.

It seems like a really nice way to wind up our voyage, with new friends and no responsibilities. More people fill in, and Rä introduces us to a half

dozen Icelanders who are all extremely friendly, and I feel like I belong there. It seems that Dillon is a place with a lot of regulars. It's getting late, and we need to get up early. Everybody hugs us, and saying goodbye is harder than I thought, not just to our new friends but to the entire concept of Iceland.

We spend our final night at the Airbnb and the next morning we pack all our black sand, all our lava rocks, all our yarn and our books, all our socks and sweaters and our knitting needles, and walk to the BSÍ bus terminal, where we book a trip back to the airport, where we will get on planes, Joan to Indiana and the rest of us to Philadelphia.

"Hey! Where did you get your sweater?" asks a man in line at Customs, with a fancy folding bicycle as his only luggage.

"I made it myself," I say, feeling instantly satisfied, "while traveling around the Ring Road."

Coda

A few weeks later, I get an email from Védís with a lot of attachments. Intrigued by our conversation, she's gone back through newspaper archives and scanned a bunch of articles for us. One of them is the 1998 *Vikan* magazine interview with Auður Laxness where she claims to have created the first lopapeysa. It has a number of intriguing photos, but it's entirely in Icelandic. I email it to Hera, who's in New Zealand on tour, and the next day, between radio interviews, she calls and reads it to me in English over the phone.

Hera's voice is measured, careful, and mellifluous, her accent halfway between New Zealand and Iceland. It's hard not to feel sad hearing her talk about Auður and thinking about the quiet house by Helgufoss that we visited with Mikael. The article starts with a photo of Auður: loose gray curls piled on her head, umbrella in one hand, purse clutched under the other arm, smiling, as though a friend had just stopped her on the way from the car to say hello.

"It's peaceful in the Mosfellsdalnum," Hera begins. "The widow of Halldór Laxness goes swimming in the pool at the house, which she does daily as long as it's not too windy. Auður says her life has not changed after Halldór's passing, other than that, she doesn't go to the nursing home at Reykjalund daily. 'I used to visit Halldór every day,' she says. She has enough to do during the day. Recently there were two French women here making a documentary about Halldór, and people from overseas are always coming every now and then. 'It always rains letters on me, there are so many letters every day. Many people don't realize that Halldór is dead. I try and answer every letter, but I've recently stopped answering requests about autographs.'"

Hera skips around, looking for the things that might be interesting.

"And then the author of the article," says Hera in an aside, "tells us that the magazine got a telephone call from someone who said that Auður Laxness had invented the lopapeysa and *Vikan* sent this person out to ask her about it. *So, they ask her, did you invent the lopapeysa?* And she says, *Yes, that would be right,* and goes on to say that in the late 1930s, there were a glut of books about knitting sweaters and they mostly used a waffle pattern, which is one knit and one purl, but in 1943, Halldór brought her a book that he'd picked up on a trip to South America. In this book were pictures of Incan clothing. And then the magazine says," continues Hera, quoting now, "The patterns on the lopapeysa which we always thought were completely, strongly Icelandic, are not Icelandic—they've come from the Incas, discovered by the Nobel Prize-winning author in an American book and then adapted by the artist Auður Svendaughter.'"

I wonder if they're giving Halldór too much credit here.

"Auður knitted a sweater with this pattern," says Hera, saying a few words in Icelandic to herself a few times and trying to figure out how to relay the meaning, "Her sister, who she says was the first woman to learn goldsmithing in Iceland, made the buttons out of... *tveggjeyringum*... I think that's *coins*. The buttons were made from coins. And she wore that sweater skiing for years. It was red with yellow and khaki, and then..." Hera reads ahead, "it says she knitted sweaters for friends and for people visiting, and she knitted several for Halldór,

The Inca pattern that started it all.

LOPA-peysa

þar sem umf. byrjar. Aukið út á síð-
ustu umf. 8 l. með jöfnu millibili.
Takið ermaprjón nr. 5 og prjónið
sléttprjón 6 umf. í sama lit. Skiptið
um lit (mynstur eftir skýringar-
mynd) og aukið út nú og í 5. hverri
umf. þannig: Prjónið 1 l. aukið í með
því að prjóna tvisvar í næstu l. (Fyrst
framan í síðan aftan í), prjónið þar
til 2 l. eru eftir af umf., aukið þá í
aftur á sama hátt, prjónið 1 l. Gætið
þess að mynstur haldist rétt annars
staðar en á útaukningsstöðum, þar
sem það eðlilega raskast nokkuð. Þeg-
ar jafnlangt er komið í mynstri á
ermi og á bol, dragið upp á band 6
miðl. undir hendi.

Nú eru 50 l. á hvorri ermi og á bol
64 l. sitt hvoru megin við úrtökul.
Alls 228 l. Setjið saman bol og ermar
á stóra hringprjóninn og setjið enn
merki þar sem bolur og ermar mæt-
ast. Prjónið 1 umf. skv. munstri.
Takið nú úr fyrir laskaermunum þannig: Byrjið á bol (þar sem umf. byrjar)
vinstra megin við merki. Prjónið 1 l.
takið 2 saman sl., prjónið þar til 3 l.
eru eftir að næsta merki. (Takið þá
eina l. óprj., prjónið næstu og steypið

6   HUGUR OG HÖND

Hugur og Hönd **magazine, June 1966.**

but he never wore one. And then she says that if anybody knitted a lopi like this before 1943, she'd love to hear about it.... When they ask her about the development of the lopi since then, she says it's been good and that they're beautiful jumpers but that personally she's really over it, she's sick of lopapeysas but still makes them when someone in the family asks because it's quick and they're fun. Then she gives the interviewers hot apple cake with whipped cream, and on the way out the door, they ask her if she's gone anywhere lately. And she says she went to Denmark recently, to the place that she and Halldór used to go twice a year because she wanted to see what had changed and that was all she needed to do; she'll never travel again. 'I'm completely done, seeing everything in this big world,' she tells them, 'I don't really care what day I die, but I feel I've finished my role.' And that's it," says Hera, "That's the end. They include a photo of the Inca pattern that she took the design from that was in the book."

And there's also a photo of Auður, wearing her first sweater with the pattern around the neck, the one with raglan sleeves.

I flip through the other things that Védís sent, articles that talk about people coming to Iceland to buy sweaters, one about American soldiers buying them to take home, one by Auður, in 1950, lamenting that most of the sweaters people sell to tourists are garbage. But one sticks out, it's a clipping from *Hugur og Hönd* magazine, the journal of the Icelandic Handcraft Society. The article is from 1966 and includes a sweater pattern called *LOPA-peysa*. It's a thickly knit colorwork sweater with six stripes and contrasting rows of tick marks and ... *raglan sleeves*.

"To be a lopapeysa or not to be a lopapeysa," Védís has written underneath, "that is the question."

KNITTING THE LOPAPEYSA

You've read about our adventures; now are you ready to try knitting your own lopapeysa? If you're feeling apprehensive, I'm here to help!

First, if you're unfamiliar with the lopapeysa, or yoked sweaters in general, here's a handy schematic.

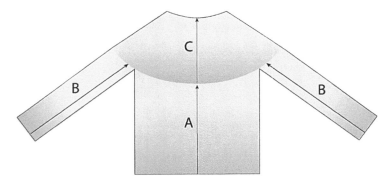

Anatomy of an Icelandic Sweater
A: BODY; knit from hem to underarm.
B: SLEEVES; knit from cuff to underarm.
C: YOKE; knit from underarm to neck.

The Icelandic lopapeysa is typically knit from the bottom up, with the sleeves knit separately and then attached at the yoke, which is generally where all the fun patterns come into play.

The neat thing about knitting a sweater in one piece versus knitting each part separately and seaming it together at the end is that you can try it on as you go. It's very easy to customize and make your lopi work for you.

In this book, there are 12(ish) patterns (some patterns, like the Adventure Sweater, are really two patterns in one), ranging from easy to difficult. The patterns are all rated, so you know what you're getting into before you cast on:

Beginner: If you know how to cast on, bind off, knit, and purl, you can do this pattern.
Advanced Beginner: You know how to do everything in beginner, plus some increasing, decreasing, and changing colors.
Intermediate: Things start getting a little spicy! You can do everything listed in the above skills plus chart reading and stranded colorwork.
Experienced: You can do all of the above as well as picking up stitches, hoods, complex colorwork, and more advanced construction.

Don't be too intimidated by the difficulty level. Each pattern will lay out what techniques are used as well as special stitches. Read through everything, and then pick up your needles and go!

Here are some facts about knitting lopapeysa colorwork and construction. Almost all of your colorwork will be in the round. It looks intimidating if you've never done it before, but it's actually very simple to work. If you are unsure, or you've never done colorwork at all before, start small with the "Learn to Chart Headbands," which will have you working with two-color knitting but back and forth. This will also give you a great template for creating your own design.

Ready to try a project in the round but not ready to dive into a full sweater? The Executioner's Capelet is a great jumping-off point—bulky yarn, big needles, stranded colorwork, but much shorter and less time-consuming than a lopapeysa sweater. There is also the Hot Springs Hat, perfect for working a simple chart pattern for the first (or second or third) time.

Recipes versus Patterns

I've heard knitters talk over and over again about their favorite "recipes" for their lopapeysa sweater. I have decided that I like that word better than "pattern" when talking about knitting. "Pattern" seems concrete, something you follow that is repetitive. "Recipe" sounds like more what knitting actually is for me. My grandmother gave me a piece of paper with instructions on how to make a cardigan. I knit it but maybe changed the sleeves, the length, the construction. Her basic idea was great, but I changed it to fit my life. And I do the same thing with her recipe for cherry pie. I don't want to use animal lard (ew, Grandma!), so I use butter. It's a recipe; it can change to fit your current lifestyle.

Other knitters have it explained even further. Most people refer to the "recipe" as the body of something and the "pattern" as the actual designs you're putting into the yoke. So you might take your favorite sweater recipe but follow the yoke pattern from another sweater.

Sizing

Talking about recipes is a good place to talk about sizing. Sometimes things need to be adjusted, and we've tried to make it easy. Standard sizing says that if someone is a 2XL versus an XS, then we not only adjust the bust size but also the length of the body and the arms. However, that's not always the case. So just remember that if you're a 2XL bust but on the shorter side overall, there's no reason that you can't adjust how long you knit a sweater or its sleeve. Also pay attention to negative versus positive ease. A sweater with negative ease will be a tighter fit. If you would like something a little more relaxed, size up. This is also an important place to mention that when we talk gauge swatching, you should block your swatch for the most accurate measurement!

Cardigans and Steeking

For the uninitiated, steeking can seem scary. I've seen experienced knitters balk at the thought of taking scissors to their long-toiled-over projects. In every project I've worked in America that required steeking, I was always told to take the "more is better" approach: four to six stitches knit into the area to be cut, alternating colors. In Iceland, minimalism seems to be key. "Four stitches?" asked Margrét at the co-op when I asked about how she steeks a cardigan compared to how I steek a cardigan. "I do one, sometimes two [purl] stitches." Over and over, every Icelander I asked repeated that they don't do any more than 2 purl stitches for a steek. So that is what I wrote into the patterns for these lopapeysas. It worked for every single one I made, with no issue. But if you're worried, or you prefer a bigger steek, just remember that knitting is organic, patterns are just recipes, and it's your sweater, so you can do whatever you want.

HOW TO STEEK

Pssst... want to know a big secret? If you're knitting with wool, especially a sticky wool like Icelandic wool, you don't actually *need* to reinforce a steek. Yarn doesn't want to unravel horizontally. So once you cut between your purl stitches, you could just add in your zipper or crochet button band, and your sweater will be just fine. If the mere thought of that is giving you the cold sweats, reinforce that steek! Do it two different ways, whichever makes you feel better.

After you've blocked your sweater and woven in the ends (away from your purl stitches please!) you'll be ready to steek. Blocking is a really important part of sweater knitting and shouldn't be skipped. I can't tell you the number of times I've despaired at the way a sweater looks, only to be perfectly happy with it once it's been blocked. Not only that, blocking can help with moth prevention, which is essential when knitting with pure wool.

There are several methods for reinforcing. The second simplest (The first simplest is paying someone to do it for me. Zero shame. I like knitting; I am not a huge fan of sewing) that I've found is to reinforce your steek by machine-sewing stitches through each of your steek (purl) stitches. Cut (with your sharpest fabric scissors, not the ones you use to break down cardboard boxes) right down the center of your two purl stitches, in between those reinforcements.

Don't have a sewing machine? Don't worry, you can still steek. Use the sharpest yarn needle or

Reinforcing both sides of the purl stitches.

When reinforcing, make sure you're going through the stitch with your tapestry needle.

Cut through your purl stitches with your sharpest fabric scissors.

Reinforcing with a crochet hook.

embroidery needle at your disposal and a yarn smaller than what your project was knit with. (Einband is great for reinforcing a steek.) Insert your needle and yarn into the stitch as if you were splitting it, scoop some of that stitch up, and then do the same into the stitch above. Go all the way up the side of your steek (yes, it'll take you a few minutes) then turn and come back down, this time backstitching around each stitch. Do that for the other side, and then cut.

Feel like whipping out some good old-fashioned crochet hooks? Reinforcing the steek with crochet is fun and oddly satisfying. Use a crochet hook one size down from the needle size that you used. And again, it's a good idea to use a smaller size yarn that what you knit your project with.

With your project facing you, make a slipknot and place it on your crochet needle. Single crochet onto your cast-on edge, and then work up the left-hand side of your steek stitches, working a single crochet around the leg of your steek stitches. When you get to the top, chain 4 and bind off. Work back down the other side. Chain 4 and bind off.

Steek all done? Next is deciding how you want to close your cardigan. Knitting a button band and sewing it on is always an option, as well as picking up stitches and knitting the button band directly onto your sweater. However, besides a sewn-on zipper (again, no shame in paying someone to do this if you don't enjoy sewing!), the most popular seems to be a crochet button band. You'll find directions for that in the Lakeside Lopapeysa pattern (p. 129). It's simple to do and probably the fastest way to finish a sweater.

One small note: I often block before cutting a steek and after putting on a button band. (There's no need with a sewn in zipper.) It just helps your final sweater look a little more put together.

Yarn

Let's talk about the yarn you'll be using. Of course, we are only using authentic Icelandic wool for this book. If you substitute, wool is best for projects that are going to be steeked. Otherwise, just ensure that your gauge is correct.

Icelandic sheep grow two types of wool, a soft inner insulating fiber and an outer layer that protects them from the wind and rain. This makes for an excellent sweater, as the yarn produced from this wool tends to have natural water-resistant qualities. However, it can make the wool itchy, especially if you have sensitive skin. There are conditioners made for wool that you can wash your sweater in to soften the fibers, or you can simply wear it over other layers, as most people in Iceland do.

Ístex is the main manufacturer of yarn in Iceland. Their yarn is everywhere. Seriously. We went to a store that sold guitars, knives, and Ístex yarn.

We used the following Ístex yarns in this book:

Einband: Laceweight. You can knit with Einband by itself or with another yarn. Or hold two strands of Einband together. It starts out stiff but softens after washing.

Léttlopi: This and Álafoss Lopi are the yarns used for patterns in this book. Usually easiest to buy and import to the United States, Léttlopi is a wonderful "workhorse" yarn and available in a variety of colors. It's a lightweight yarn in Iceland

Holding yarn in each hand makes it easy to switch colors.

The dominant color (the main part of this colorwork pattern) is in the left hand.

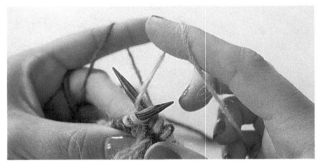

Work stitches from right or left needle to follow colors as shown on your chart.

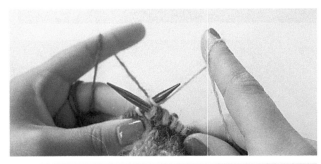

The back side of your stranded colorwork should look nice and even, almost as pretty as the front!

but comparable to a worsted weight yarn in other parts of the world.

Álafoss Lopi: A bulky weight yarn, it knits up very quickly and is great for a fast sweater. My Álafoss Lopi sweaters tend to be my outdoor winter sweaters, while my Léttlopi sweaters get worn around the house or on breezy fall days.

There are other Ístex yarns, which Kyle talks about in the travel section of this book. All of them are lovely to knit with in different ways. Find the one that works best for your project. When working with yarn that is either unspun or only lightly spun, you may experience breakage. But don't worry, since it is wool, you can simple wet felt it back together. A little moisture and friction and your two pieces of yarn will become one again with very little effort. If you notice your yarn is continually breaking, you may consider adjusting your tension and ensure that you aren't pulling your stitches too tightly. Not only can that break your yarn but it can make for an oddly shaped finished knit.

Speaking of tension, if you're just diving into stranded knitting, here are some tips!

- Relax those hands! If your tension is too tight, the color pattern will be tighter than the rest of your piece. Wiggle your fingers, shake your hands, dip your toes in warm water, and imagine the beauty of Iceland if you need to.
- Keep your yarn untangled. Every few rounds, check your yarn to make sure that it is not a knotted mess. (Try saying "not a knotted mess" four times fast; that will also help you relax!)
- Most lopapeysas don't have you carrying one color for more than five stitches; however, sometimes it is unavoidable (see Hestaland Horse Sweater and Puffin Sweater). When that happens, just ensure that you twist the yarn within that five stitches so that your floats (those strands of yarn at the back of your work) don't get too long.
- Always hold your dominant color to the left, and ensure you do that for the entire project. If you're holding one color in each hand, the dominant color should be in your left hand, and the background color in your right hand.

Needles

Like yarn, needles can make a difference. If you're using authentic Icelandic wool, you may find that wooden or bamboo needles get pretty sticky to work with, especially around the yoke. They will work, and if that is what you have, there is no need to go out and buy new ones. However, if you have metal needles on hand, you may find them easier for knitting your lopapeysa.

You'll want to use circular needles, as you'll almost always be knitting in the round, and even if you aren't, circular needles are easiest when working with a lot of stitches, even flat ones (such as in the Waiting Cape on p. 143). Always choose a circular needle with a nice flexible cable and a smooth join. You'll usually need two lengths, one longer circular needle for the body and then a shorter one for the decreases in the yoke and neck.

Double-pointed needles are the standard for sleeves, but of course you can use whichever method you prefer for working in the round. I often use a longer circular needle and employ a version of the magic loop method, because I can't always be bothered to get up and find the correct double-pointed needle set.

Abbreviations

You should be familiar with most of the abbreviations in this book, but just in case, they're listed here:

BO	Bind off
CH	Crochet chain stitch
CO	Cast on
Dec	Decrease
Inc	Increase
K	Knit
K2tog	Knit 2 stitches as 1
Kf&b	Knit into the front and the back of a stitch
M1	make one stitch (increase)
M1L	make one left. With your left needle, go from front to back into the strand between your two stitches. Use your right needle to knit through the back of the loop.
M1R	make one right. With your left needle, go from back to front into the strand between your two stitches. Knit through the front of the loop.
P	Purl
PM	Place Marker
RS	Right side of work
SC	Single crochet
SM	Slip Marker
Ssk	Slip, slip, knit
WS	Wrong side of work

Important Skills

Of course, you need to know some basic knitting to do the patterns in this book. But a few other important knitting techniques are necessary as well.

GRAFTING

Sometimes called the Kitchener stitch, grafting is a seamless way of closing live stitches. It's used for every underarm in the book and also used to seam hoods. Here's a quick tutorial on grafting if you've never done it before:

You must have an even number of stitches, divided evenly between two needles (or split on one circular needle).

With both points facing forward, cut a 12 in. (30.5 cm) tail and thread it onto a yarn needle.

1. Insert the yarn needle through the stitch on the knitting needle closest to you as if to purl, and pull it through. Leave the stitch on the needle.
2. Insert the yarn needle through the stitch on the knitting needle farthest from you as if to knit, and pull it through. Leave the stitch on the needle.
3. Insert the yarn needle through the stitch on the knitting needle closest to you as if to knit, and pull it off the needle.
4. Insert the yarn needle through the next stitch on the knitting needle closest to you as if to purl, and leave it on the needle.
5. Insert the yarn needle through the stitch on the knitting needle farthest from you as if to purl, and pull it off the needle.
6. Insert the yarn needle through the next stitch on the knitting needle farthest from you as if to knit, and leave it on the needle.
7. Repeat steps 3 to 6 until all stitches have been worked.

CHART READING

When reading a chart in the round, always start on the right side of the chart for each round worked.

Two patterns in this book will be worked flat. For those charts, work back and forth: row 1 right to left and row 2 left to right.

The chart key will tell you when you're knitting, purling, decreasing, and what color yarn you're using. Make sure to take a look at it before starting your project.

If this is your first time knitting lopapeysas, I can't tell you how excited I am for you to start your journey! Make one, and then make a dozen because they're absolutely fun and addictive to knit!

LEARN TO CHART HEADBAND

Diving into a lopapeysa chart for the first time can be a little intimidating. This basic headband pattern is intended to teach you the basics of knitting from a chart for the first time.

For this headband, you will knit back and forth, which means reading the chart from right to left on the first row, then left to right on the next row. This is different from a yoke chart, which is read from right to left each time. It also utilizes a provisional cast-on. Using either a spare cable needle or waste yarn, you'll cast on, leaving the stitches "live" so that you can graft them together later.

There are two different versions of this headband. The Whale is knit in the lighter Léttlopi, while the Heart is shown in the heavier Álafoss Lopi. This is a great chance to try a small project with two different weights of lopi yarn to see the difference yarn can make!

Difficulty Level
Intermediate

Skills Required
Provisional cast-on
Knit and purl stitches
Grafting
Reading a chart
Increasing, decreasing
Stranded colorwork

Materials

For Whale Headband

YARN
Léttlopi (100% wool; 109 yds/100 m per
1.75 oz/50 g ball)
- MC: #0054/Ash Heather; 1 ball
- CC: #1403/Lapis Blue Heather; 1 ball

NEEDLES
US size 9/5.5 mm straight needles

For Heart Headband

YARN
Álafoss Lopi (100% wool; 109 yds/100 m per
3.5 oz/100 g ball)
- MC: #0159/Orchid; 1 ball
- CC: #1240/Dark Magenta; 1 ball

NEEDLES
US size 10½/6.5 mm

Materials for Both
Tapestry needle
Waste yarn or spare circular needle (the size is not
    particularly important; just ensure the cable is
    long enough so it's not in danger of falling out)
4 stitch markers

Gauge
Whale Headband: 18 stitches/20 rows =
4 in/10 cm square in stockinette stitch using
US 9/5.5 mm needles
Heart Headband: 14 stitches/16 rows =
4 in/10 cm square in stockinette stitch using
US 10½/6.5 mm needles

Size
One size

Finished Measurements
Whale Headband: 4.5 in/11.5 cm at widest point;
22 in/56 cm around
Heart Headband: 5 in/13 cm at widest point;
21.5 in/54.5 cm around

Special Stitches

PROVISIONAL CAST-ON

This should feel very similar to a long tail cast-on. Start with either tying your waste yarn and working yarn in a knot together or placing a slipknot on the spare cable needle. This will not count as a stitch.

1. Set up with the cable or waste yarn on top, your working yarn on the bottom, and your working needle in your right hand.
2. Move the needle down in front of the cable/waste yarn, pick up your working yarn, and lift up in front of the needle.
3. Move the needle down behind the cable needle or waste yarn and pick up the working yarn.
4. Repeat steps 2 and 3 until you have all stitches on both your cable needle/waste yarn and working needle.

1X1 RIB

Row 1: Knit 1, purl 1.
Row 2: Knit 1, purl 1.

KF&B (KNIT FRONT AND BACK)

1. Knit into your stitch, but do not take it off the needle.
2. Knit into the back of the stitch; then remove from the needle as you normally would.

Instructions

BOTH HEADBANDS

Using the provisional cast-on, CO 10 sts.
Row 1: (K1, p1) twice, pm, k2, pm, (k1, p1) twice.
Row 2: (K1, p1) to marker, sm, p to marker, sm, (k1, p1) twice.
Row 3 (Inc Row): (K1, p1) to marker, sm, (kf&b) twice, sm, (k1, p1) twice. 12 sts
Row 4: Work row 2.
Row 5 (Inc Row): Work 1x1 rib to marker, kf&b, k to 1 st before marker, kf&b, sm, 1x1 rib to end. 14 sts
Work rows 4 and 5 (ending with row 4) until 20 sts are on your needle.
Begin working from either Whale or Heart Chart, as desired.

Next row: 1x1 rib to marker, sm, p to marker, sm, 1x1 rib to end.
Next row: 1x1 rib to marker, sm, k to marker, sm, 1x1 rib to end.
Next row: 1x1 rib to marker, sm, p to marker, sm, 1x1 rib to end.
Begin decreases:
Row 1 (Dec Row): Work 1x1 rib to marker, sm, ssk, k to 2 sts before marker, k2tog, sm, work 1x1 rib to end.
Row 2: 1x1 rib to maker, sm, p to marker, sm, 1x1 rib to end.
Repeat these 2 rows until 10 sts remain.

FINISHING

Graft ends together. Weave in ends.

Whale Chart

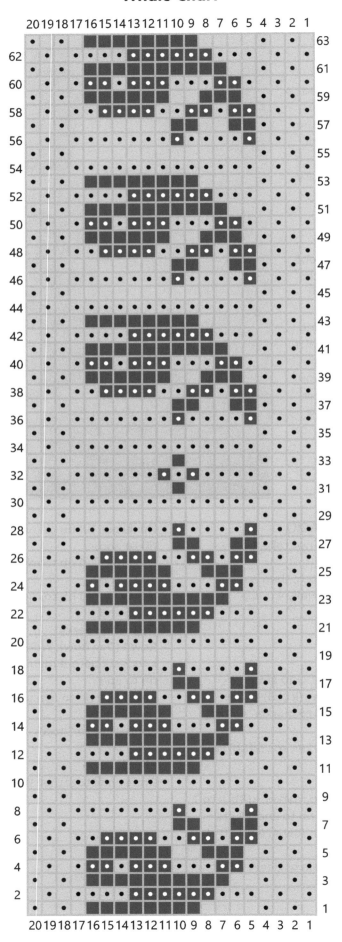

Heart Chart

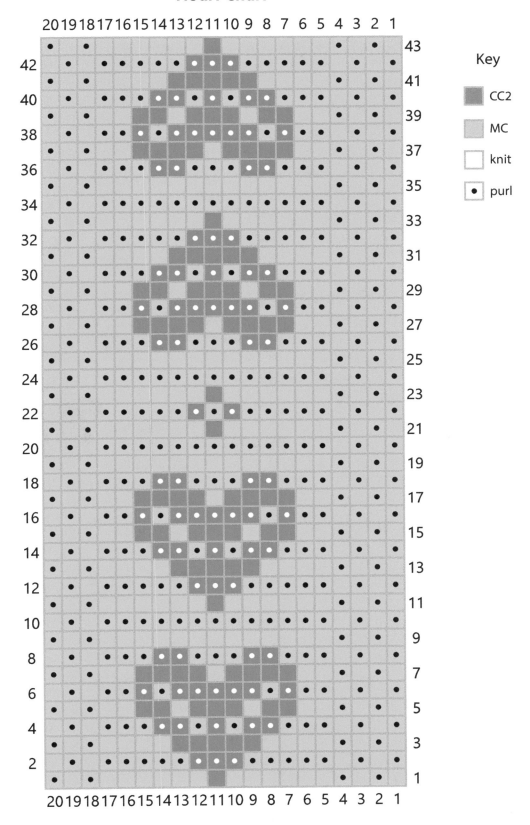

HOT SPRINGS HATS

While the water in the hot springs is, well, hot, the air outside is still cold. That means every part of you that is in the water is perfectly comfortable, but you're going to want to keep your head warm.

This pattern is designed for your hot springs adventure. Knit in pure Icelandic wool, with an easy-to-follow stranded knitting pattern, this is a great beginner project!

These hats are designed to keep your head warm, even with a cold Icelandic breeze. Knit in the round, there are two pattern variations available. Hat 2 will be more fitted, while Hat 1 is a little bit slouchier. As you become more skilled, feel free to design your own color pattern.

And once you get comfortable, check out the bonus fishie chart. Just plug it in on either Hat 1 or Hat 2.

Difficulty Level
Intermediate

Skills Required
Knit and purl, cast-on
Knitting in the round
Stranded colorwork
Increasing, decreasing
Working from chart

Materials

YARN
Léttlopi (100% wool; 109 yd/100 m per
1.75 oz/50 g ball)

Hat 1
• MC: #9420/Navy Blue; 1 ball

Hat 2
• MC: #1402/Heaven Blue; 1 ball

Both Hats
• CC1: #0057/Grey Heather; 1 ball
• CC2: #9432/Grape Heather; 1 ball
• CC3: #1402/Heaven Blue; 1 ball

NEEDLES
US 7/4.5 mm 16 in/40 cm circular needle
US 8/5 mm 16 in/40 cm circular needle
US 8/5 mm double-pointed needles or preferred
    needles for working a small circumference
    in the round

NOTIONS
Stitch marker
Yarn needle

Gauge
20 stitches/25 rows = 4 in/10 cm using US 7
(4.5 mm) needles in stockinette stitch
18 stitches/26 rows = 4 in/10 cm using US 8 (5 mm)
needles in stockinette stitch

Sizes
Medium: fits 21–22 in/53–56 cm head
(Large): fits 23–24 in/58–61 cm head

Finished Measurements

Hat 1
Circumference: 21.5 in/54.5 cm
Depth: 9 in/22 cm from crown to brim edge

Hat 2
Circumference: 21.5 in/54.5 cm
Depth: 7.5 in/19 cm from crown to brim edge

Special Stitches

1X1 RIB STITCH
Knit 1 stitch, purl 1 stitch all the way around.

2X2 RIB STITCH
Knit 2 stitches, purl 2 stitches all the way around.

Instructions

BOTH HATS
With smaller needle and MC, CO 108 (120) sts; join in the round, taking care not to twist the stitches. Place marker to indicate the start of the round.

HAT 1
Work 2x2 rib for 10 (12) rounds.
Switch to larger circular needles.
Work Hot Springs Hat Chart rows 1–8 twice.

HAT 2
Work 1x1 rib for 10 (12) rounds.
Switch to larger circular needles.
Work Hot Springs Hat Chart rows 1–8 once.

HAT 1
Knit around for 14 (16) rounds.

HAT 2
Knit around for 10 (12) rounds.

BOTH HATS

Begin decrease rounds (switch to dpns when necessary):
Round 1: (K10, k2tog) around. 99 (110) sts
Round 2: Knit around.
Round 3: (K9, k2tog) around. 90 (100) sts
Round 4: Knit around.
Round 5: (K8, k2tog) around. 81 (90) sts
Round 6: Knit around.

HAT 1

Round 7: (K7, k2tog) around. 72 (80) sts
Round 8: Knit around.
Round 9: (K6, k2tog) around. 63 (70) sts
Round 10: Knit around.
Round 11: (K5, k2tog) around. 54 (60) sts
Round 12: Knit around.
Round 13: (K4, k2tog) around. 45 (50) sts
Round 14: (K3, k2tog) around. 36 (40) sts
Round 15: (K2, k2tog) around. 27 (30) sts
Round 16: (K1, k2tog) around. 18 (20) sts
Round 17: (K2tog) around until 6 sts remain.

HAT 2

Round 7: (K7, k2tog) around. 72 (80) sts
Round 8: (K6, k2tog) around. 63 (70) sts
Round 9: (K5, k2tog) around. 54 (60) sts
Round 10: (K4, k2tog) around. 45 (50) sts
Round 11: (K3, k2tog) around. 36 (40) sts
Round 12: (K2, k2tog) around. 27 (30) sts
Round 13: (K1, k2tog) around. 18 (20) sts
K2tog around until 6 sts remain.

FINISHING (BOTH HATS)

Break yarn, leaving a 12 in (30.5 cm) tail. Thread through remaining stitches.
Weave in ends and block.

Hot Springs Hat Chart

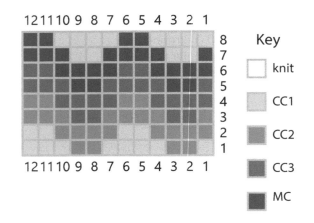

Key
- knit
- CC1
- CC2
- CC3
- MC

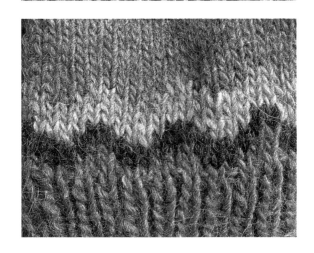

Bonus Chart

I used this hat recipe to make a gift for a friend but substituted a fish pattern. She loved it so much she told me I should include the chart in the book. So here it is, in case you have a fishie-loving friend as well!

Hot Springs Hat Fishie Chart

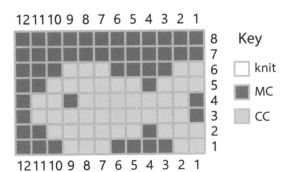

Key

- ☐ knit
- ■ MC
- ☐ CC

EXECUTIONER'S CAPELET

Agnes Magnúsdóttir was the last person to be executed in Iceland, in 1830. This capelet is less inspired by that event and more inspired by the location of the event. The brisk winds you feel as you read a sad history and climb a hill to the execution site make you want to wrap yourself up in something warm.

The pattern is for two sizes: Small/Medium and Large/XL. If you want to make it even larger, simply add increase rounds to match the chart (8 stitches for Chart 1 and 12 stitches for Chart 2). This piece is knit from the bottom up, with decreases worked in the chart for the top. Like the Hot Springs Hats, it's a great way to practice stranded knitting!

Difficulty Level
Intermediate

Skills Required
Knit and purl, cast on and bind off
Increasing, decreasing
Knitting in the round on a circular needle
Garter stitch in the round

Materials

YARN
Álafoss Lopi (100% wool; 109 yds/100 m per
3.5 oz/100 g ball)
- MC: #1241/Gloxinia; 2 (3) balls
- CC1: #1240/Dark Magenta; 1 (1) ball
- CC2: #0159/Orchid; 1 (1) ball

NEEDLES
US 13/9 mm 24 in/60 cm circular

NOTIONS
Stitch marker

Gauge

12 sts/14 rounds = 4 in/10 cm square in stockinette stitch using US 13/9 mm needles

Sizes

Small/Medium (Large/XL)

Finished Measurements

Height: 14 (14.5) in/35.5 (36.83) cm
Width: 40 (48) in/101.6 (121.9) cm around at widest point

Special Stitches

1X1 RIB

Knit 1, purl 1 around.

GARTER IN THE ROUND

Round 1: Knit around.
Round 2: Purl around.
Repeat these 2 rounds.

Instructions

With MC, CO 120 (144) sts; join to work in round.
Work 8 rounds of garter stitch.
Knit around for 4 rounds.
Begin working from Chart 1.
Knit 4 (6) rounds.
Begin working from Chart 2.
For size Small/Medium: Work rounds 1–23.
For size Large/XL: Work all rounds.
After dec round 18: 100 (120) sts
After dec round 22: 80 (96) sts
Size L/XL only, after dec round 24: (72) sts
Work 1x1 rib for 6 rounds.
Bind off in pattern.

Executioner's Capelet Chart 1

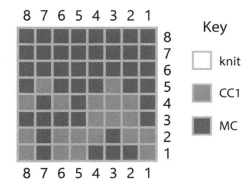

Executioner's Capelet Chart 2

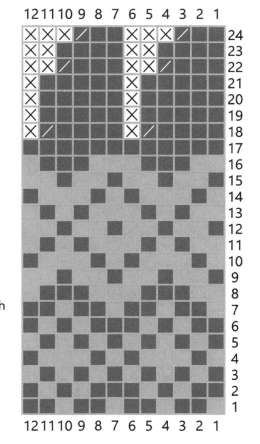

Key

EVERYWHERE SWEATER

Ready to attempt your first lopapeysa? This one is very easy! Knit it as a cardigan if you're feeling brave, or simply eliminate those two purl stitches and knit it as a pullover. I decided to call this the Everywhere Sweater as we wore these everywhere! Volcano, glacier, hot springs—every version of this got worn by most of our motley crew as we trekked around Iceland.

The yoke pattern is designed to be easy for someone just dipping their toes into the stranded knitting water. If you make a small mistake in the colorwork, chances are no one will ever notice.

A helpful tip: when checking your stitch counts, don't forget your two steeking purl stitches are included in your count (if you're making the cardigan version).

Difficulty Level
Intermediate

Skills Required
For the Pullover:
- Knit and purl, cast on and bind off
- Increasing
- Working in the round on circular needles
- Working in the round on double-pointed or small-circumference needles
- Working from a chart
- Grafting

For the Cardigan (in addition to above):
- Steeking

Materials

YARN
Álafoss Lopi (100% wool; #109 yd/100 m per 3.5 oz/100 g ball)
- MC: #0056 Ash Heather; 5 (5, 5, 6, 6, 7) balls
- CC1: #9959 Indigo; 2 (2, 2, 2, 3, 3) ball
- CC2: #1232 Arctic Exposure; 1 ball
- CC3: #0057 Grey Heather; 1 ball

NEEDLES
US size 9/5.5 mm 16 in/40 cm circular needles
US size 9/5.5 mm 32 in/81 cm circular needles
US size 9/5.5 mm double-pointed needles
US size 10½/6.5 mm 16 in/40 cm circular needles
US size 10½/6.5 mm 32 in/81 cm circular needles
US size 10½/6.5 mm double-pointed needles

NOTIONS
Stitch marker
Yarn needle
Zipper with two sides, appropriate to size (20–22 in/51–56 cm), for Cardigan

Gauge
14 sts/18 rounds = 4 in/10 cm square in stockinette stitch using US 10½/6.5 mm needles
16 sts/20 rounds = 4 in/10 cm square in stockinette stitch using US 9/5.5 mm needles

Sizes
XS (S, M, L, XL, 2XL, 3XL)

Finished Measurements
Chest: 33.75 (37, 43, 46, 52, 56.5, 65.7) in/85.7 (94, 109, 117, 132, 143.5, 167) cm
Length to underarm: 17.5 (18, 18.5, 19, 19.5, 20, 20.5) in/44.5 (45.7, 47, 48.25, 49.5, 51, 52) cm
Sleeve to underarm: 18 (19, 19.5, 20, 20, 20.5, 20.5) in/45.7 (48.25, 49.5, 51, 51, 52, 52) cm

Special Stitches

2X2 RIB
Knit 2, purl 2 around.

1X1 RIB
Knit 1, purl 1 around.

Pattern Note
If you would like to make this as a pullover instead of a cardigan, just eliminate the first 2 purl sts on each round.

Instructions
With smaller, longer circular needle and CC1, CO 118 (130, 150, 162, 182, 198, 230).
Place marker and join to work in the round.
Purl 2, work 2x2 rib to end.
Repeat this round a total of 10 times.
With larger needles, work from Chart 1.
With MC, work in stockinette stitch (maintaining purl sts for cardigan) until piece measures 17.5 (18, 18.5, 19, 19.5, 20, 20.5) in/44.5 (45.7, 47, 48.25, 49.5, 51, 52) cm from cast-on edge. Set aside and begin sleeves.

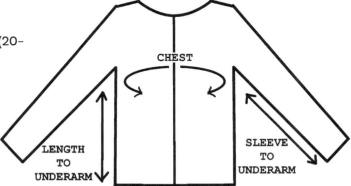

Chest: 33.75 (37, 43, 46, 52, 56.5, 65.7)"/
85.7 (94, 109, 117, 132, 143.5, 167)cm

Length to Underarm: 17.5 (18, 18.5, 19, 19.5, 20, 20.5)"/
44.5 (45.7, 47, 48.25, 49.5, 51, 52)cm

Sleeve to Underarm: 18 (19, 19.5, 20, 20, 20.5, 20.5)"/
45.7 (48.75, 49.5, 51, 51, 52, 52)cm

SLEEVES (MAKE 2)

With smaller double-pointed needles or preferred method for working in the round and CC1, CO 28 (32, 32, 36, 36, 36, 36) sts.

Work from Chart 2.

With larger dpns and MC, knit 1 round.

Inc Round: K1, m1, k to end of round, m1. 30 (34, 34, 38, 38, 38, 38) sts

Knit 4 rounds.

Repeat the last 5 rounds 8 (8, 9, 9, 10, 11, 11) more times, switching to circular needles when necessary. 46 (50, 52, 56, 58, 60, 60) sts

Knit around until sleeve measures 18 (19, 19.5, 20, 20, 20.5, 20.5) in/45.7 (48.25, 49.5, 51, 51, 52, 52) cm.

Slip 8 (8, 8, 8, 8, 8, 10) sts to holder.

YOKE

With larger, longer circular needle and MC, purl 2, k25 (28, 33, 36, 41, 45, 57), sl 8 (8, 8, 8, 8, 8, 10) sts to holder, k38 (42, 44, 48, 50, 52, 50) sleeve sts, k50 (56, 66, 72, 82, 90, 114) from back, sl 8 (8, 8, 8, 8, 8, 10) sts to holder, k38 (42, 44, 48, 50, 52, 50) from other sleeve, k25 (28, 33, 36, 41, 45, 57). 178 (198, 222, 242, 266, 286, 310) sts

Next round: Knit around, increasing 0 (2, 0, 2, 0, 2, 0). 178 (200, 222, 244, 266, 288, 310) sts

Begin working from Chart 3, switching to shorter circular needles when necessary.

Stitch counts after dec rounds:

After round 17: 162 (182, 202, 222, 242, 262, 282) sts

After round 21: 146 (164, 182, 200, 218, 236, 254) sts

The Everywhere Sweater

Chart 1

24 23 22 21 20 19 18 17 16 15 14 13 12 11 10 9 8 7 6 5 4 3 2 1

16 15 14 13 12 11 10 9 8 7 6 5 4 3 2 1

24 23 22 21 20 19 18 17 16 15 14 13 12 11 10 9 8 7 6 5 4 3 2 1

Chart 2

4 3 2 1

8 7 6 5 4 3 2 1

4 3 2 1

Key

☐ knit

▨ CC3

■ CC2

▦ CC1

☐ MC

• purl

☒ no stitch

╱ k2tog

☐ Repeat

After round 30: 130 (146, 162, 178, 194, 210, 226) sts
After round 34: 114 (128, 142, 156, 170, 184, 198) sts
After round 36: 82 (92, 102, 112, 122, 132, 142) sts
After round 39: 66 (74, 82, 90, 98, 106, 114) sts
With MC, purl 2, work 1x1 rib around for 6 rounds.
BO in pattern.

FINISHING
Weave in all ends and graft underarms. When weaving in ends, make sure you're weaving away from your steek stitches.

Set Up the Steek
Either machine sew or hand sew small straight stitches twice through each set of purl stitches. Cut between the sewn rows.
Set in and sew zipper, or follow the instructions for the Lakeside Lopapeysa for a crochet button band (see p. 129).

The Everywhere Sweater
Chart 3

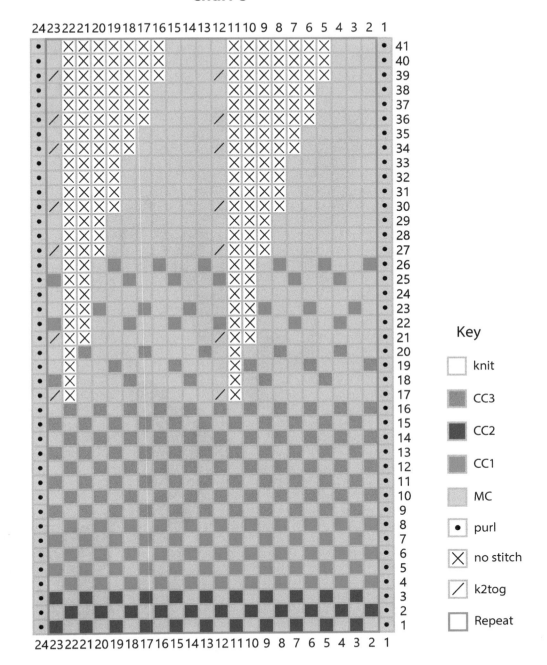

Key

- ☐ knit
- ⬜ CC3
- ⬛ CC2
- ⬜ CC1
- ☐ MC
- • purl
- ☒ no stitch
- ╱ k2tog
- ☐ Repeat

ICELANDIC HORSE SWEATER

The Icelandic horse (don't call them ponies—it hurts their feelings) is one of the purest breeds in the entire world. It is the only horse you will find in Iceland, as no other horse is allowed in the country. And once you take an Icelandic horse out of Iceland, it can never come back. If you're even a mild horse enthusiast, you should make the trek to ride one during your trip. We spent our time at Hestaland, which is only a half hour from Reykjavik. Our journey to Hestaland actually started in Indiana. At my daughter's swim class, a woman next to me noticed I was knitting. I mentioned I was working on a book about Icelandic knits and heading there in a few weeks. Turns out she was as well, because her brother-in-law owns a horse farm called Hestaland! How could we not meet up after a magic encounter like that? (PS: you'll also find the mom herself, the gorgeous Ali, modeling the Lakeside Lopapeysa on p. 124, and her son August modeling the toddler version of the Puffin Sweater on p. 122). At Hestaland, you can ride for a day or stay on the property and ride for a week! This sweater showcases the iconic Icelandic horse on the yoke. The decreases are worked around the tree in the chart, making them part of the colorwork pattern.

Most stranded sweaters avoid working more than five stitches of one color in a row; however, sometimes this cannot be avoided. When working the horses, either make sure you are twisting your yarn every five stitches, to avoid your floats being too long, or focus on carrying the yarn loosely to avoid it bunching up.

Difficulty Level
Intermediate

Skills Required
Knit and purl, cast on and bind off
Increasing, decreasing
Working in the round on circular needles
Working small circumferences in the round on
    dpns/magic loop/two circulars
Working from charts
Stranded colorwork
Grafting

Materials

YARN
Álafoss Lopi (100% wool;109 yds/100 m per
3.5 oz/100 g ball)
· MC: #0085/Oatmeal Heather; 6 (6, 6, 6, 7, 7) balls
· CC1: #0058/Dark Grey Heather; 2 (2, 2, 3,
    3, 3) balls
· CC2: #0052/Black Sheep; 1 (1, 2, 2, 2, 2) balls
· CC3: #1233/Space Blue; 1 (1, 1, 1, 1, 1) ball
· CC4: #1237/Sheep Sorrel; 1 (1, 1, 2, 2, 3) balls

NEEDLES
US size 10½/6.5 mm 32 in/80 cm circular needles
Set of four US size 10½/6.5 mm dpns or preferred
    needles for working in the round
US size 10½/6.5 mm 16 in/40 cm circular needles
US size 11/8 mm 32 in/80 cm circular needles
Set of four US size 11/8 mm dpns or preferred
    needles for working in the round

NOTIONS
Stitch marker
Yarn needle
6 stitch holders or waste yarn

Gauge
16 sts/20 rounds = 4 in/10 cm
square in stockinette stitch
using US 10½/6.5 mm needles
14 sts/18 rounds = 4 in/10 cm
square in stockinette stitch using
US 11/8 mm needles needles

Sizes
XS (S, M, L, XL, 2XL)

Finished Measurements
Chest: 45 (50, 54, 59, 64, 68) in/114 (127, 137, 150,
162.5, 173) cm
Length to underarm: 18 (18.5, 19, 19.5, 20, 21) in/45.7
(47, 48.25, 49.5, 51, 53) cm
Sleeve to underarm: 15.5 (16, 16.5, 16.5, 17, 18) in/39
(40.5, 42, 42, 43, 45.7) cm

Pattern Note
This sweater has 3 in/7.5 cm of positive ease. For
a more fitted sweater, choose one size down from
what you would normally wear.

Special Stitches

1X1 RIB
Knit 1, purl 1 around.

2X2 RIB
Knit 2, purl 2 around.

Instructions

BODY
With MC and smaller circular needle, CO 104 (124,
136, 152, 164, 176) sts.
Place marker and join to work in the round.
Work 2x2 rib for 8 rounds.
Switch to larger circular needle.
Knit around until piece measures 18 (18.5, 19, 19.5,
20, 21) in/45.7 (47, 48.25, 49.5, 51, 53) cm from
cast-on edge.
Set aside and make sleeves.

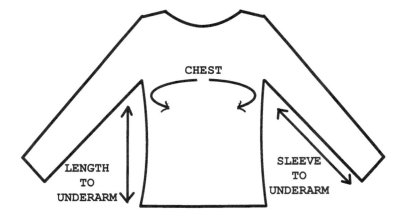

Chest: 45 (50, 54, 59, 64, 68)"/
114 (127, 137, 150, 162.5, 173)cm

Length to Underarm: 18 (18.5, 19, 19.5, 20, 21)"/
45.7 (47, 48.25, 49.5, 51, 53)cm

Sleeve to Underarm: 15.5 (16, 16.5, 16.5, 17, 18)"/
39 (40.5, 42, 42, 43, 45.7)cm

Icelandic Horse Sweater Chart

Column numbers (top): 16 15 14 13 12 11 10 9 8 7 6 5 4 3 2 1

Row numbers (right side): 40 through 1

Column numbers (bottom): 16 15 14 13 12 11 10 9 8 7 6 5 4 3 2 1

Key

☐	knit
■ (CC4)	CC4
■ (CC3)	CC3
■ (CC2)	CC2
☐ (CC1)	CC1
⊠	no stitch
⧄	k2tog
⧅	ssk

SLEEVES (MAKE 2)

With MC and smaller double-pointed needles, CO 22 (26, 26, 30, 34, 40) sts, place marker and join in the round, taking care not to twist the sts.

Work 1x1 rib for 6 rounds.

Switch to larger double-pointed needles.

Knit around for 5 rounds.

Inc round: K1, m1, k to marker, m1. 24 (28, 28, 32, 36, 42) sts

Repeat these 6 rounds 8 (9, 10, 10, 11, 11) times more to 40 (46, 48, 52, 54, 60) sts. Switch to shorter circular needle when necessary.

Knit around until sleeve measures 15.5 (16, 16.5, 16.5, 17, 18) in/39 (40.5, 42, 42, 43, 45.7) cm.

Slip 6 (10, 10, 12, 12, 14) sts at beginning of round to holder for underarm. 34 (36, 38, 40, 42, 46) sts per sleeve. Place live stitches on waste yarn or stitch holder while working second sleeve.

YOKE

With MC and larger, longer circular needles, knit 22 (26, 30, 34, 38, 37) sts across right front of body. Place next 6 (10, 10, 12, 12, 14) sts on holder for underarm. Knit 34 (36, 38, 40, 42, 46) sts of first sleeve. Knit across 48 (52, 56, 60, 64, 74) back sts, place next 6 (10, 10, 12, 12, 14) sts on holder for underarm, knit across 34 (36, 38, 40, 42, 46) sts of second sleeve, knit remaining 22 (26, 30, 34, 38, 37) sts. 160 (176, 192, 208, 224, 240) sts

Knit 2 rounds and begin working from Chart. Switch to shorter circular needle when necessary.

Stitch counts after dec rounds:

After round 21: 150 (165, 180, 195, 210, 225) sts

After round 28: 130 (143, 156, 169, 182, 195) sts

After round 32: 110 (121, 132, 143, 154, 165) sts

After round 35: 100 (110, 120, 130, 140, 150) sts

After round 36: 80 (88, 96, 104, 112, 120) sts

After round 38: 60 (66, 72, 78, 84, 90) sts

With MC, switch to smaller circular needle, work 1x1 rib for 4 rounds. Bind off in pattern.

FINISHING

Graft underarms. Weave in all ends and block.

Icelandic Horse Sweater Chart

PUFFIN SWEATER

Puffins are well known in Iceland. Not necessarily the brightest of birds, they are incredibly cute. We got glimpses of them on our whale watch in Hauganes and again in the cliffs of Vik.

This sweater is knit in the round and sized for both toddlers and adults. Both use the same chart for the sleeves and lower body but different charts for the yoke, as the toddler decreases differ from the adult sizes.

Difficulty Level
Intermediate

Skills Required
Knit and purl, cast on and bind off
Increasing, decreasing
Working small circumferences in the round on
   dpns/with magic loop/with two circulars
Stranded knitting
Working from a chart
Wrangling a toddler into a sweater

Materials

YARN
Álafoss Lopi (100% wool; 109 yds/100 m per
3.5 oz/100 g ball)
- MC Toddler: #1231/Garden Green; 2 (2, 3) (0, 0, 0,
  0, 0, 0) balls
- MC Adult: #1238/Dusk Red; 0 (0, 0) (6, 6, 7, 8,
  8, 9) balls
- CC1: #0085/Oatmeal Heather; 0 (0, 0) (1, 1, 2, 2,
  2, 2) balls
- CC2: #9964 Golden Heather; 1 (1, 1) (1, 2, 2, 2,
  2, 2) balls
- CC3: #0059/Black; 1 (1, 1) (1, 2, 2, 3, 3, 3) balls
- CC4: #0051/White; 1 (1, 1) (1, 2, 3, 3, 3, 3) balls
- CC5: #0118/Navy; 1 (1, 1) (1, 2, 2, 3, 3, 3) balls

NEEDLES
For adult sizes:
US size 9/5.5 mm 32 in/80 cm circular needle
US size 10½/6.5 mm 32 in/80 cm circular needle

For both sizes:
US size 9/5.5 mm double-pointed needles
   or preferred method for working small
   circumferences in the round
US size 9/5.5 mm 16 in/40 cm circular
   needle
US size 10½/6.5 mm double-
   pointed needles or preferred
   method for working small
   circumferences in the round

For toddler sizes:
US size 9/5.5 24 in/60 cm
   circular needle
US size 10½/6.5 mm 24 in/60 cm
   circular needle

NOTIONS
6 stitch holders or waste yarn
Stitch marker
Yarn needle

Gauge
13 sts/19 rounds = 4 in/10 cm square in stockinette
stitch using US 10½/6.5 mm needles
14 sts/30 rounds = 4 in/10 cm square in stockinette
stitch using US 9/5.5 mm needles

Sizes
2T (3T, 4T) (XS, S, M, L, XL, 2XL)

Finished Measurements
Chest: 22.25 (24.5, 29.5) (44.25, 46.75, 51.75, 56.5,
59, 64) in/56.5 (62, 75) (112.4, 118.7, 131.4, 143.5,
150, 162.5) cm
Length to underarm: 8 (8.5, 9) (16, 16, 17, 17.5, 18, 19)
in/20 (21.5, 23) (40.5, 40.5, 43, 44.5, 45.7, 48.25) cm
Sleeve to underarm: 8 (8, 8.25) (17.5, 18, 18.5, 19, 20,
21) in/20 (20, 21) (44.5, 45.7, 47, 48.25, 51, 53) cm

Pattern Note
This sweater is designed with 2 in/5 cm positive
ease. For a more fitted sweater, choose one size
down from your normal size.

Special Stitches

1X1 RIB
Knit 1, purl 1 around.

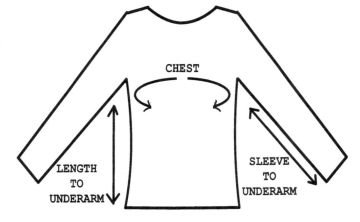

Chest: 22.25 (24.5, 29.5) (44.25, 46.75, 51.75, 56.5, 59, 64)"/
56.5 (62, 75) (112.4, 118.7, 131.4, 143.5, 150, 162.5)cm

Length to Underarm: 8 (8.5, 9) (16, 16, 17, 17.5, 18, 19)"/
20 (21.5, 23) (40.5, 40.5, 43, 44.5, 45.7, 48.25)cm

Sleeve to Underarm: 8 (8, 8.25) (17.5, 18, 18.5, 19, 20, 21)"/
20 (20, 21) (44.5, 45.7, 47, 48.25, 51, 53)cm

Instructions

With smaller circular needles (24 in/60 cm for toddler and 32 in/80 cm for adult) and MC as applicable, CO 72 (80, 96) (144, 152, 168, 184, 192, 208) sts.

PM and join to work in the round.

Work 1x1 rib for 2 in/5 cm.

With larger circular needles, knit 2 rounds.

Begin working from Body Chart.

For toddler sizes, replace CC1 with MC, as shown in Toddler Key.

With MC, knit around until piece measures 8 (8.5, 9) (16, 16, 17, 17.5, 18, 19) in/20 (21.5, 23) (40.5, 40.5, 43, 44.5, 45.7, 48.25) cm from cast-on edge.

SLEEVES (MAKE 2)

With MC and smaller double-pointed needles, CO 20 (24, 28) (32, 32, 36, 40, 44, 48) sts.

Place marker and join to work in the round.

Work 1x1 rib for 2 in/5 cm.

With larger double-pointed needles, knit 1 round.

Begin working from Sleeve Chart.

For toddler sizes, replace CC1 with MC, as shown in Toddler Key.

With MC, knit 1 round.

Inc round: K1, m1, k to last st, m1.

Puffin Sweater

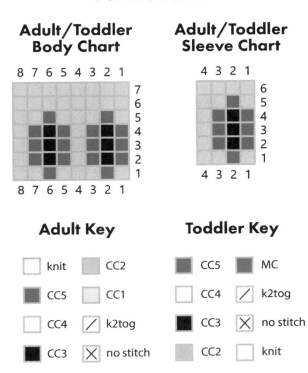

Adult/Toddler Body Chart

Adult/Toddler Sleeve Chart

Adult Key

- ☐ knit
- ■ CC5
- ☐ CC4
- ■ CC3
- ▨ CC2
- ☐ CC1
- ◢ k2tog
- ⊠ no stitch

Toddler Key

- ■ CC5
- ☐ CC4
- ■ CC3
- ▨ CC2
- ■ MC
- ◢ k2tog
- ⊠ no stitch
- ☐ knit

Knit 3 (4, 4) (5, 5, 5, 5, 5, 5) rounds plain. 22 (26, 30) (34, 34, 38, 42, 46, 50) sts

Repeat the last 4 (5, 5) (6, 6, 6, 6, 6, 6) rounds 5 (4, 4) (5, 6, 6, 5, 7, 10) more times. 32 (34, 38) (44, 46, 50, 52, 60, 70) sts

Knit around until sleeve measures 8 (8, 8.25) (17.5, 18, 18.5, 19, 20, 21) in/20 (20, 21) (44.5, 45.7, 47, 48.25, 51, 53) cm; place 7 (7, 8) (8, 9, 10, 10, 11, 12) sts on holder.

Place remaining sleeve stitches on holder or waste yarn.

YOKE

With MC and larger, longer circular needle, k14 (16, 20) (32, 33, 37, 41, 42, 46), sl 7 (7, 8) (8, 9, 10, 10, 11, 12) sts to holder, k25 (27, 30) (36, 37, 40, 42, 49, 58) sleeve sts, k across 30 (34, 40) (64, 68, 74, 82, 86, 92) back sts, sl 7 (7, 8) (8, 9, 10, 10, 11, 12) sts to holder, k25 (27, 30) (36, 37, 40, 42, 49, 58) sleeve

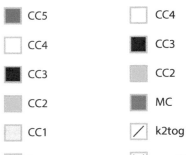

Puffin Sweater Yoke

Adult

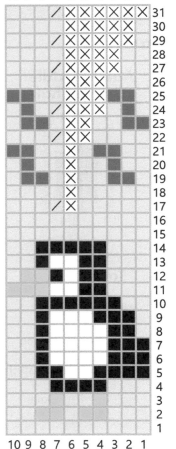

Toddler

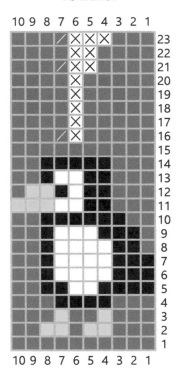

Adult Key

☐	knit
■	CC5
☐	CC4
■	CC3
■	CC2
☐	CC1
╱	k2tog
☒	no stitch

Toddler Key

■	CC5
☐	CC4
■	CC3
■	CC2
■	MC
╱	k2tog
☒	no stitch
☐	knit

sts, k14 (16, 20) (32, 33, 37, 41, 42, 46). 108 (120, 140) (200, 208, 228, 248, 268, 300) sts
Increase 2 (0, 0) (0, 2, 2, 2, 2, 0) across back. 110 (120, 140) (200, 210, 230, 250, 270, 300) sts
Knit 1 round.
Begin working from Adult or Toddler Yoke Chart, switching to smaller circular needles when circumference becomes too small.
Stitch counts after Toddler Yoke decreases:
After round 16: 99 (108, 126) sts
After round 20: 88 (96, 112) sts
After round 22: 77 (84, 98) sts
After round 24: 66 (72, 84) sts
After round 25: 55 (60, 70) sts
Stitch counts after adult yoke decreases:
After round 17: 180 (189, 207, 225, 243, 270) sts
After round 22: 160 (168, 184, 200, 216, 240) sts
After round 24: 140 (147, 161, 175, 189, 210) sts
After round 27: 120 (126, 138, 150, 162, 180) sts
After round 29: 100 (105, 115, 125, 135, 150) sts
After round 31: 80 (84, 92, 100, 108, 120) sts

Adult sizes only:
Knit 1 round.
K2, k2tog around.
Knit 1 round.
K2, k2tog around.
Knit 1 round.

All sizes:
With smaller, shorter circular needles k1, p1 around for 1 in/2.5 cm.
Bind off in pattern.

FINISHING
Graft underarms, weave in all ends.
Block.

LAKESIDE LOPAPEYSA

On our first trip to Iceland, we couldn't help but fall in love with all the different bodies of water. One memorable day, we went out to a cave next to a lake, and our friend Kiddi taught us all how to skip stones. We were all chilly from being in and near the water, and I found myself envying the cardigans I saw our local friends wearing. I knew I had to make my own, inspired by the day we spent by the lake!

Knit in Léttlopi, from the bottom up, this pattern incorporates two purl stitches that will be reinforced on either side and then steeked (cut). I used a crochet button band, but you can also sew in a zipper or use a knit button band if you prefer. The CC1 and CC2 colors are in such small amounts that you can easily use a half ball of something you have sitting around in your stash.

I've included two charts with this pattern. I wanted to show how just little changes can be incorporated within the same chart to change the look. Chart 1 has four colors in the yoke (main color and three contrasting colors). Chart 2 was simplified to just three colors (main color and two contrasting colors). It's fun to play with charts. Change colors, add some spots of color—do what you want to make this recipe yours!

Difficulty Level
Advanced

Skills Required
Knit and purl, cast on and bind off
Increasing, decreasing
Working in the round on circular needles
Working from charts
Stranded colorwork
Steeking
Crochet
Grafting

Materials

YARN
Léttlopi (100% wool; 109 yds/100 m per
1.75 oz/50 g ball)
- MC: #0054/Light Ash Heather; 6 (7, 8, 8, 9, 9) balls
- CC1: #1403/Lapis Blue Heather; 1 (1, 2, 2, 2, 2) balls
- CC2: #1402/Heaven Blue Heather; 1 (1, 1, 1, 1, 1) ball
- CC3: #1702/Heaven Blue; 1 (1, 1, 1, 1, 1) ball

NEEDLES
US size 7/4.5 mm 24 in/60 cm circular needle
US size 7/4.5 mm double-pointed needles
   or preferred method for working small
   circumferences in the round
US size 8/5 mm 24 in/60 cm circular needle
US size 8/5 mm 16 in/40 cm circular needle
US size 8/5 mm double-pointed needles
   or preferred method for working small
   circumferences in the round
Size G-6/4.25 mm crochet hook

NOTIONS
3 stitch markers
6 stitch holders or waste yarn
Tapestry needle
6 split stitch markers or safety
   pins for marking buttonholes
6 ⅝ in/16 mm buttons
Corresponding thread and
   sewing needle

Gauge
18 sts/24 rounds = 4 in/10 cm square in stockinette
stitch using US 7/4.5 mm needles
16 sts/22 rounds = 4 in/10 cm square in stockinette
stitch using US 8/5 mm needles

Sizes
XS (S, M, L, XL, 2XL)

Finished Measurements
Chest: 35.5 (38, 40, 43.5, 46, 48) in/90 (96.5, 101.5,
110.5, 117, 122) cm
Length to underarm: 15 (16, 17, 17, 18, 18) in/38 (40.5,
43, 43, 45.7, 45.7) cm
Sleeve length to underarm: 17 (17.5, 18, 18.5, 19, 19.5)
in/43 (44.5, 45.7, 47, 48.25, 49.5) cm

Pattern Notes
This sweater is knit with 2 in/5 cm positive ease, so
choose one size down for a more fitted sweater.
The lopapeysa is knit in the round from the bottom
up and then steeked, with a crochet button band
added on. Should you prefer a pullover, simply
eliminate the two purl stitches.

Special Stitches

2X2 RIB
Knit 2 stitches, purl 2 stitches around for
each round.

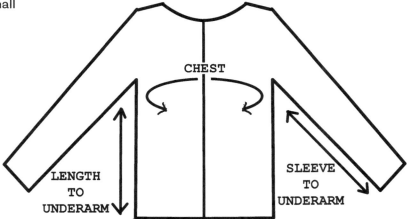

Chest: 35.5 (38, 40, 43.5, 46, 48)"/
90 (96.5, 101.5, 110.5, 117, 122)cm

Length to Underarm: 15 (16, 17, 17, 18, 18)"/
38 (40.5, 43, 43, 45.7, 45.7)cm

Sleeve to Underarm: 17 (17.5, 18, 18.5, 19, 19.5)"/
43 (44.5, 45.7, 47, 48.25, 49.5)cm

Instructions

BODY
With MC and smaller circular needle, CO 142 (154, 162, 174, 186, 194) sts.
Place marker and join to work in the round.
Purl 2 (these are your steeking stitches), pm, work 2x2 rib around.
Repeat for a total of 12 rounds.
Switch to larger, longer circular needle.
Purl 2, knit around.
Knit around, maintaining 2 steeking sts for 15 (16, 17, 17, 18, 18) in/38 (40.5, 43, 43, 45.7, 45.7) cm.
Set aside and begin sleeves.

SLEEVES
With MC and smaller dpns, CO 40 (48, 52, 56, 60, 64) sts.
Place marker and join, work 2x2 rib for 5 in/13 cm.
With larger dpns, knit 6 rounds.
Next round: K1, m1, k to marker, m1. 42 (50, 54, 58, 62, 66) sts
Repeat these 7 rounds 7 (6, 7, 7, 7, 7) more times. 56 (62, 68, 72, 76, 80) sts

Knit around until sleeve measures 17 (17.5, 18, 18.5, 19, 19.5) in/43 (44.5, 45.7, 47, 48.25, 49.5) cm.
Slip 12 (14, 15, 16, 16, 16) sts to holder. 44 (48, 53, 56, 60, 64) sleeve sts.

YOKE
With MC, p2, k29 (31, 32, 35, 38, 40), slip 12 (14, 15, 16, 16, 16) sts to holder, k44 (48, 53, 56, 60, 64) sleeve sts, k58 (62, 66, 70, 76, 80) from back, sl 12 (14, 15, 16, 16, 16) sts to holder, k44 (48, 53, 56, 60, 64) sleeve sts, k29 (31, 32, 35, 38, 40) sts to end.
206 (222, 238, 254, 274, 290) sts
Knit 1 round, increase 0 (1, 2, 3, 0, 1) across back.
206 (223, 240, 257, 274, 291) sts
Knit 1 round.
Work from desired Chart.
Stitch counts after chart decreases:
After round 16: 182 (197, 212, 227, 242, 257) sts
After round 27: 158 (171, 184, 197, 210, 223) sts
After round 40: 134 (145, 156, 167, 178, 189) sts
After round 43: 89 (93, 100, 107, 114, 121) sts
Bind off.

Lakeside Lopapeysa
Chart 1

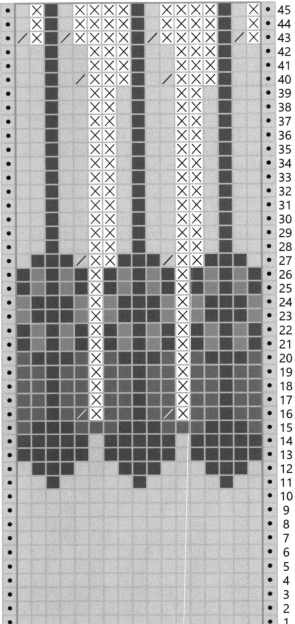

Lakeside Lopapeysa
Chart 2

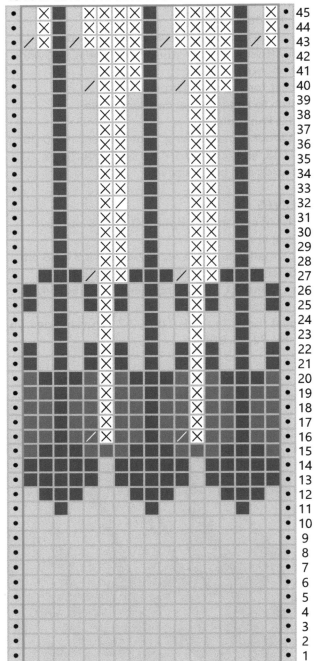

Key

☐	knit	▨	MC
•	purl	■	CC1
☒	no stitch	▨	CC3
╱	k2tog	■	CC2

FINISHING

Graft underarm sts together and weave in all loose ends. Sew by machine or hand through each set of purl sts up front of body. Cut carefully between the rows. (See p. 87 for tips on steeking.)

Right Band

With right side facing, use crochet hook and MC (or CC1, if you prefer) and single crochet in every other knitted row up the right side, ch1, turn.
Next row: Sc in every stitch across.
Work 2 more rows of single crochet.
Cut yarn and pull through.

Left Band

With right side facing, use crochet hook and MC (or CC1, if you prefer) and single crochet in every other row up the left side, ch1, turn.
Mark where you would like your buttonholes.
Our sample has them every 4 in/10 cm, or 13 sts, but you can do more or less, depending on your preference; just make sure they are evenly spaced.
Use split stitch markers or safety pins to mark buttons opposite buttonholes.
Next row: Single crochet to marker, ch2, sc to next marker, ch2, repeat to end of row.
Single crochet two more rows; cut yarn and pull through.
Sew your buttons using corresponding thread where you have placed your stitch markers.
Block.

HIKING GLOVES

A pair of warm gloves is a must for Iceland. Even in July, we found ourselves pulling on these gloves to get warm on a misty hike. Made from hearty wool, these have some fun color worked into the fingers. If that's not to your taste, you can knit them in a solid color, but for all except the smallest size, you will need one additional ball of yarn in the main color. The nice thing about the colorwork is it can be done with leftover scraps from other projects! Try them on as you knit the fingers to make sure you get the length that works for you.

There are a few different ways to play with color with these gloves. As shown in our photos, you can simply use the contrasting color to work the fingers, or you can follow the instructions for striping on the fingers in the pattern.

Difficulty Level
Advanced Beginner

Skills Required
Knit and purl, cast on and bind off
Increasing, decreasing
Working small circumferences in the round on
 dpns/with magic loop/with two circulars
Picking up stitches
Knitting and purling through the back loop

Materials

YARN
Léttlopi (100% wool; 109 yds/100 m per
1.75 oz/50 g ball)
- MC: #1701/Fjord Blue; 1 (1, 2)* balls
- CC1: #1700/Air Blue; 1 (1, 1) balls

*Note: If you choose to knit these in a solid color
instead of two colors, you will need an additional
ball of MC for sizes medium and large.

NEEDLES
US size 8/5 mm double-pointed needles
 or preferred needles for working small
 circumferences in the round.

NOTIONS
Stitch marker
4 stitch holders or waste yarn
Tapestry Needle

Gauge
20 sts/24 rounds = 4 in/10 cm square in
stockinette stitch using US 8/5 mm needles

Sizes
S (M, L)

Finished Measurements
Small: 7.5 in/19 cm cuff, 8 in/20 cm length
(Medium): 8.5 in/21.5 cm cuff, 9 in/23 cm length
(Large): 8.75 in/22 cm cuff, 9 in/23 cm length

Special Stitches

HALF TWISTED RIB
1. Knit the first stitch through the back loop.
2. Bring the yarn between the needles to the front.
3. Purl the next stitch normally.
4. Bring the yarn between the needles to the back of the stitch.
5. Repeat steps 1 to 4 for half twisted rib stitch.

Pattern Notes
These gloves are knitted from the bottom cuff up, with a thumb gusset added by doing increases; then the top of the glove is split in half, and live stitches are picked up to knit the fingers. There will be seaming at the end to close off the gaps in between each finger.

One of my favorite glove-knitting hacks: When you cut the tail for your index fingers, leave a long tail. That way if, after decreasing, you decide you need the finger a little bit longer, you can add a few more rounds.

Instructions

BOTH GLOVES
With MC, CO 36 (42, 46) sts. Join without twisting, and place marker to work in the round.
Work half twisted rib for 12 (14, 14) rounds.
Knit around for 5 (7, 9) rounds.
Inc Round: K1, m1, k to end of round, m1. 38 (44, 48) sts
Next round: Knit around.
Repeat these two rounds 4 (4, 5) times more. 46 (52, 58) sts
Next round: Knit to 4 (4, 5) sts before marker.

THUMB GUSSET
Slip 4 (4, 5) sts before and after marker onto stitch holder. Remove marker.
Cast on 2 (2, 4) sts over thumb gusset gap, pm and join. 40 (46, 52) sts
Knit around for 12 (12, 14) rounds.
Next round: K15 (18, 20), slip next 10 (10, 12) sts to holder, CO 1 st across gap. Knit to end of round. 31 (37, 41) sts
Knit around for 3 (3, 5) rounds.

INDEX FINGER
Next round: K5 (6, 7), slip next 11 (12, 14) sts to a holder or waste yarn (left-side holder), then slip next 10 (12, 13) sts (right-side holder). CO 1 st across

gap. Knit to end. Reposition on needles and begin index finger. 11 (14, 15) sts
Knit around for 13 (14, 15) rounds or desired length.
Decrease: K2tog around until 2 sts remain; cut yarn and pull through.

MIDDLE FINGER
Slip 5 (6, 6) sts from left holder and 5 (7, 7) sts from the right holder.
With MC, knit across 5 (6, 6) sts, CO 1 to close gap, k5 (7, 7), CO 1. 12 (15, 15) sts
Knit around for 2 (2, 2) rounds.
With CC, knit around for 3 (3, 3) rounds.
With MC, knit around for 1 (1, 1) round.
With CC, knit around for 1 (1, 1) round.
With MC, knit around for 8 (9, 10) rounds or desired length.
Decrease: K2tog around until 2 sts remain; cut yarn and pull through.

RING FINGER
Slip 6 (6, 7) sts from left holder and 5 (6, 7) sts from right holder.
With CC, knit across 6 (6, 7) sts, CO 1 to close gap, k5 (6, 7), CO 1 to close gap. 13 (14, 16) sts
Knit around for 5 (5, 5) rounds.
With MC, knit around for 3 (3, 3) rounds.
With CC, knit around for 6 (7, 8) rounds or desired length.
Decrease: K2tog around until 2 sts remain; cut yarn and pull through.

LITTLE FINGER
Slip remaining 10 (10, 12) sts to needles; with CC, pick up and k2 (3, 3) sts by ring finger. 12 (13, 15) sts
With CC, knit around for 12 (13, 14) rounds or desired length.
Decrease: K2tog around until 2 sts remain; cut yarn and pull through.

THUMB
Slip 8 (8, 10) sts from holder to needle. With CC, pick up and knit 4 (4, 5) sts around thumb gusset. 12 (12, 15) sts
Knit around for 10 (11, 12) rounds or desired length.
Decrease: K2tog around until 2 sts remain; cut yarn and pull through.

FINISHING
Weave in all ends. Seam gaps between fingers. Block.

ADVENTURE SWEATER

In the introduction, we talked about the different kinds of Icelandic yarn. This sweater is the perfect chance to see what a difference the type of yarn you use makes! Version 1 is knit in Álafoss Lopi. It kept me warm on the black sands beach of Katla and up and down a rainy hike to the hot springs.

Version 2 (pictured in the cave) is knit in Léttlopi. It went on many a hike as well as into the water at the Grjótagjá Cave (which, incidentally, was a very easy way to block a sweater!).

Notice how the same chart looks very different when knit with two different yarns. If you like the hood we made for Version 1, add one to Version 2. These sweaters are the perfect way to showcase the way small changes can make a big difference in your lopapeysa.

VERSION 1

Difficulty Level
Experienced

Skills Required
Knit and purl, cast on and bind off
Increasing, decreasing
Working in the round on circular needles
Working from charts
Stranded colorwork
Steeking
Grafting
Crochet chain or I-cord

Materials

YARN
Álafoss Lopi (100% new wool; 109 yd/100 m per 3.5 oz/100 g ball)*
- MC: #0086/Light Beige; 5 (6, 6, 7, 7, 8, 8) balls
- CC1: #0010/Dark Denim Heather; 1 (2, 2, 3, 3, 3, 3) balls
- CC2: #0008/Light Denim Heather; 3 (3, 3, 3, 4, 4, 4) balls

*Note: If you choose to add a hood, add 1 ball in the color you choose for it. We used CC1 for this version.

NEEDLES
US size 13/9 mm 32 in/80 cm circular needle
US size 13/9 mm 16 in/41 cm circular needle
US size 13/9 mm double-pointed needles or preferred needles for working a small circumference in the round
US G-6/4.25 mm crochet hook for making drawstring
US M-13/9 mm crochet hook if making crochet button band

NOTIONS
2 stitch markers
6 stitch holders or waste yarn
Yarn needle
Zipper or 6 ⅝ in/16 mm buttons

Gauge
12 sts/16 rounds = 4 in/10 cm square in stockinette stitch using US 13/9 mm needles

Sizes
XS (S, M, L, XL, 2XL, 3XL)

Finished Measurements
Chest: 36 (40.5, 44.5, 48.5, 52.5, 56.5, 60.5) in/91.5 (103, 113, 123, 133, 143.5, 153.6) cm
Length to underarm: 17 (17.5, 18, 18.5, 18.5, 19, 19.5) in/43 (44.5, 45.7, 47, 47, 48.25, 49.5) cm
Sleeve to underarm: 18 (18.5, 19, 19.5, 20, 20.5, 21) in/45.7 (47, 48.25, 49.5, 51, 52, 53) cm

Pattern Notes
This pattern is knit from the bottom up in one piece; then it's steeked. The hood is knit flat from the sweater neck, grafted, and then seamed, with a drawstring added. The sweater has 3–4 in/7–10 cm of positive ease. If you want a more fitted sweater, choose one size down from your normal size.

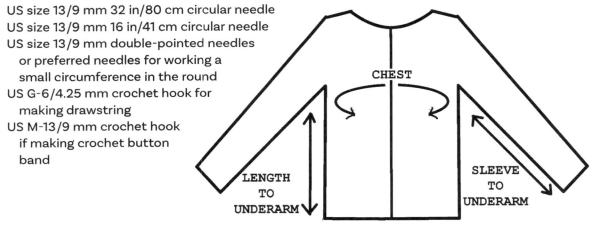

V1 measurements

Chest: 36 (40.5, 44.5, 48.5, 52.5, 56.5, 60.5)"/
91.5 (103, 113, 123, 133, 143.5, 153.6)cm

Length to underarm: 17 (17.5, 18, 18.5, 18.5, 19, 19.5)"/
43 (44.5, 45.7, 47, 47, 48.25, 49.5)cm

Sleeve to underarm: 18 (18.5, 19, 19.5, 20, 20.5, 20.5, 21)/
45.7 (47, 48.25, 49.5, 51, 52, 53)cm

Adventure Sweater
Version 1 Chart

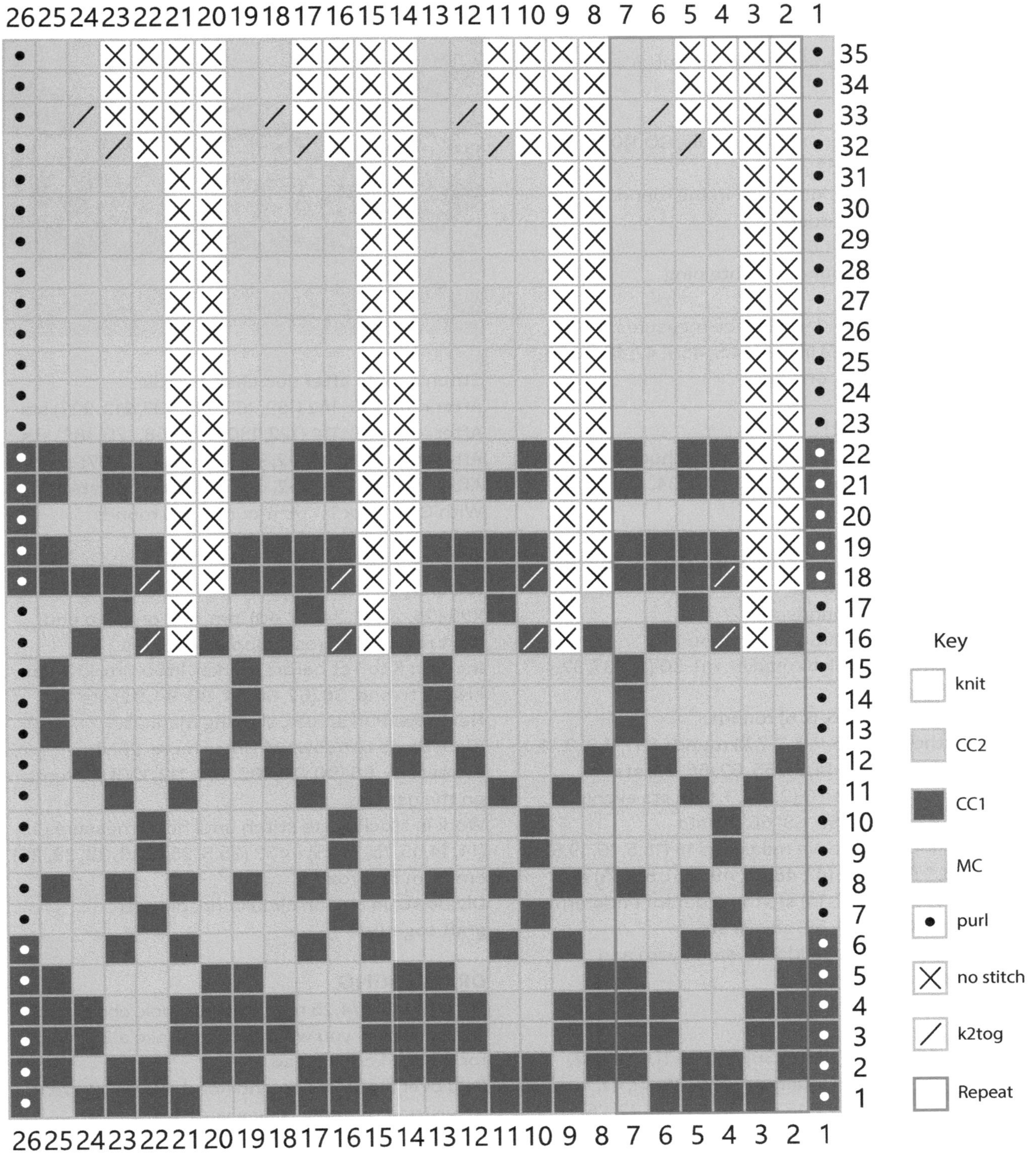

Key
- ☐ knit
- ▨ CC2
- ▦ CC1
- ▨ MC
- • purl
- ✕ no stitch
- ╱ k2tog
- ☐ Repeat

Special Stitches

1X1 RIB
Knit 1, purl 1 around.

KF&B
Knit into the front and back of the stitch.

Instructions
With CC1 and longer circular needle, CO 110 (122, 134, 146, 158, 170, 182).
Place marker and join to work in the round.
Purl 2, work 1x1 rib around.
Repeat for a total of 6 rounds.
Knit around for 5 rounds, maintaining steek stitches.
With MC, knit around until piece measures 17 (17.5, 18, 18.5, 18.5, 19, 19.5) in/43 (44.5, 45.7, 47, 47, 48.25, 49.5) cm from cast-on edge.

SLEEVES (MAKE 2)
With CC2 and dpns or preferred method for working in the round CO 28 (28, 34, 34, 42, 42, 48) sts.
Work 1x1 rib for 6 rounds.
Knit 1 round, increasing 0 (0, 1, 1, 0, 0, 1) st. 28 (28, 35, 35, 42, 42, 49) sts
Knit around for 6 rounds.
Switch to MC, knit around for 6 rounds.
Next round: K1, m1, k to marker, m1. 30 (30, 37, 37, 44, 44, 51) sts
Knit next 5 (5, 6, 6, 6, 6, 6) rounds.
Repeat the last 6 (6, 7, 7, 7, 7, 7) rounds 6 (7, 7, 9, 9, 11, 11) more times. 42 (44, 51, 55, 62, 66, 73) sts
Next round: Increase 0 (2, 1, 3, 1, 0, 0) sts evenly around. 42 (46, 52, 58, 63, 66, 73) sts
Knit around until sleeve measures 18 (18.5, 19, 19.5, 20, 20.5, 21) in/45.7 (47, 48.25, 49.5, 51, 52, 53) cm
Slip 6 (8, 11, 11, 12, 12, 14) sts to holder for underarm. 36 (38, 41, 47, 51, 54, 59) sleeve sts
Slip all sleeve sts to holder or waste yarn and begin yoke.

YOKE
P2, k24 (26, 27, 30, 33, 36, 38), sl 6 (8, 11, 11, 12, 12, 14) sts to holder for underarm, k36 (38, 41, 47, 51, 54, 59) sleeve sts, k48 (52, 56, 62, 66, 72, 76) across back, sl 6 (8, 11, 11, 12, 12, 14) sts to holder for underarm, k36 (38, 41, 47, 51, 54, 59) sleeve sts, k24 (26, 27, 30, 33, 36, 38). 170 (182, 194, 218, 236, 254, 272) sts
Knit 1 round.
Begin working from Version 1 Chart.

Stitch counts after decrease rounds:
After round 16: 142 (152, 162, 182, 197, 212, 227) sts
After round 18: 114 (122, 130, 146, 158, 170, 182) sts
After round 32: 86 (92, 98, 110, 119, 128, 137) sts
After round 33: 58 (62, 66, 74, 80, 86, 92) sts
With CC1, work 1x1 rib around for 3 rounds.
Bind off 2 purl steek stitches.

HOOD
K23 (25, 27, 31, 34, 37, 40), pm, k10, pm, k to end.
Next row: Purl across, slipping markers.
Inc row: K to 1 st before marker, kf&b, sm, k10, sm, kf&b, k to end. 58 (62, 66, 74, 80, 84, 92) sts
Next row: Purl across, slipping markers.
Work these two rows 14 times more. 28 sts increased - 86 (90, 94, 102, 108, 112, 120) sts remain on the needles.
Work in stockinette stitch until hood measures 13 (14, 14, 15, 15, 15, 15) in/33 (35.5, 35.5, 38, 38, 38, 38) cm from first row.
Divide sts in half on circular needle and graft together.

DRAWSTRING
With size G-6/4.25 mm crochet hook, chain for 20 in/51 cm; or, if you would prefer, make a 3 st I-cord for 20 in/51 cm instead.
Fold over first 5 sts around hood and sew. Thread drawstring through using a yarn needle.

FINISHING
Graft underarms.
Choose your preferred method for steeking and your preferred closure.
Block.

VERSION 2

Difficulty Level
Experienced

Skills Required
Knit and purl, cast on and bind off
Increasing, decreasing
Working in the round on circular needles
Working from charts
Stranded colorwork
Steeking

Materials

YARN
Léttlopi 100% wool; 109 yd/100 m per
1.75 oz/50 g ball)
- MC: #0085/Oatmeal; 5 (5, 6, 6, 7, 7) balls
- CC1: #1707/Galaxy; 3 (3, 3, 4, 4, 4) balls
- CC2: #0867/Chocolate Heather; 1 (1, 1, 2, 2, 2) balls

NEEDLES
US size 9/5.5 mm 32 in/80 cm circular needle and
16 in/40 cm circular needle
US size 9/5.5 mm dpns or preferred needles for
working in the round
US size J-10/6 mm crochet hook if working a
crochet button band

NOTIONS
Stitch marker
6 stitch holders or waste yarn
Yarn needle
6 ⅝ in/16 mm buttons or zipper
corresponding to finished size

Gauge
22 sts/26 rounds = 4 in/10 cm
square in stockinette stitch using
US 9/5.5 mm needles

Sizes
XS (S, M, L, XL, 2XL)

Finished Measurements
Chest: 31 (33, 35, 39.5, 42, 46) in/78.7 (84, 89, 100, 107, 117) cm
Length to underarm: 16 (16.5, 17, 17.5, 18, 19) in/40.6 (42, 43, 44.5, 45.7, 48.25) cm
Sleeve to underarm: 17 (17.5, 18, 18.5, 19, 19.5) in/43 (44.5, 45.7, 47, 48.25, 49.5) cm

Instructions
With CC1 and longer circular needles, CO 170 (182, 194, 218, 230, 254) sts.
Place marker and join to work in the round.
Purl 2, 1x1 rib around.
Repeat for 6 rounds.
Knit around for 5 rounds.
With MC, k around for 16 (16.5, 17, 17.5, 18, 19) in/40.6 (42, 43, 44.5, 45.7, 48.25) cm.

SLEEVES (MAKE 2)
Cast on 42 (48, 54, 54, 62, 62) sts.
Place marker and join to work in the round.
Work 1x1 rib around for 6 rounds.
Next round: Knit around increasing 0 (1, 1, 1, 0, 0) st at the beginning of the round. 42 (49, 55, 55, 62, 62) sts
Next round: k1, m1, k to marker, m1. 44 (51, 57, 57, 64, 64) sts

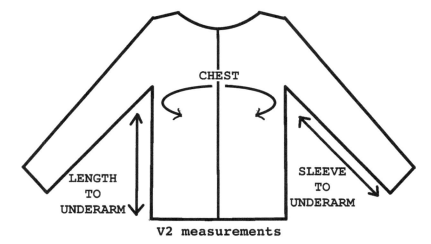

CHEST

LENGTH TO UNDERARM

SLEEVE TO UNDERARM

V2 measurements

Chest: 31 (33, 35, 39.5, 42, 46)"/
78.7 (84, 89, 100, 107, 117)cm

Length to underarm: 16 (16.5, 17, 17.5, 18, 19)"/
40.6 (42, 43, 44.5, 45.7, 48.25)cm

Sleeve to underarm: 17 (17.5, 18, 18.5, 19, 19.5)"/
43 (44.5, 45.7, 47, 48.25, 49.5)cm

Knit around for 6 rounds.
Repeat these 7 rounds 7 (7, 8, 8, 9, 8) more times.
58 (65, 73, 73, 82, 82) sts
Knit around until sleeve measures 17 (17.5, 18, 18.5, 19, 19.5) in/43 (44.5, 45.7, 47, 48.25, 49.5) cm
Place 11 (12, 13, 13, 14, 14) sts on holder for underarm,
Place remaining sts on holder or waste yarn.

YOKE
P2, k36 (39, 41, 47, 50, 56), sl 11 (12, 13, 13, 14, 14) sts to holder for underarm, k47 (53, 60, 60, 68, 68) sleeve sts, k74 (78, 84, 96, 100, 112) back sts, sl 11 (12, 13, 13, 14, 14) sts to holder for underarm, k47 (53, 60, 60, 68, 68) sleeve sts, k36 (39, 41, 47, 50, 56).
242 (264, 288, 312, 338, 362) sts
Knit 1 round, increasing 0 (2, 2, 2, 0, 0) sts. 242 (266, 290, 314, 338, 362) sts
Work from Version 2 Chart.
Stitch counts after decrease rounds:
After round 16: 200 (220, 240, 260, 280, 300) sts
After round 18: 160 (176, 192, 208, 224, 240) sts
After round 32: 120 (132, 144, 156, 168, 180) sts
After round 33: 80 (88, 96, 104, 112, 120) sts
With CC1, work 1x1 rib around for 6 rounds.
Bind off in pattern.

FINISHING
Graft underarm sts together and weave in all loose ends.

Sew by machine or hand through each set of purl sts up front of body. Cut carefully between the rows. (See p. 87 for tips on steeking.)
Choose to either sew in a zipper or follow these instructions for a crochet button band:

Right Band
With right side facing, use crochet hook and CC1 single crochet in every other knitted row up the right side, ch1, turn.
Next row: Sc in every stitch across.
Work 2 more rows of single crochet.
Cut yarn and pull through.

Left Band
With right side facing, use crochet hook and MC (or CC1, if you prefer) single crochet in every other row up the left side, ch1, turn.
Mark where you would like your buttonholes. Our sample has them every 4 in/10 cm, or 13 sts, but you can do more or less, depending on your preference; just make sure they are evenly spaced. Use split stitch markers or safety pins to mark where you want to place your buttons opposite the buttonholes.
Next row: Single crochet to marker, ch2, sc to next marker, ch2, repeat to end of row.
Sc two more rows, cut yarn and pull through.
Sew your buttons using corresponding thread where you have placed your stitch markers.
Block.

Adventure Sweater
Version 2 Chart

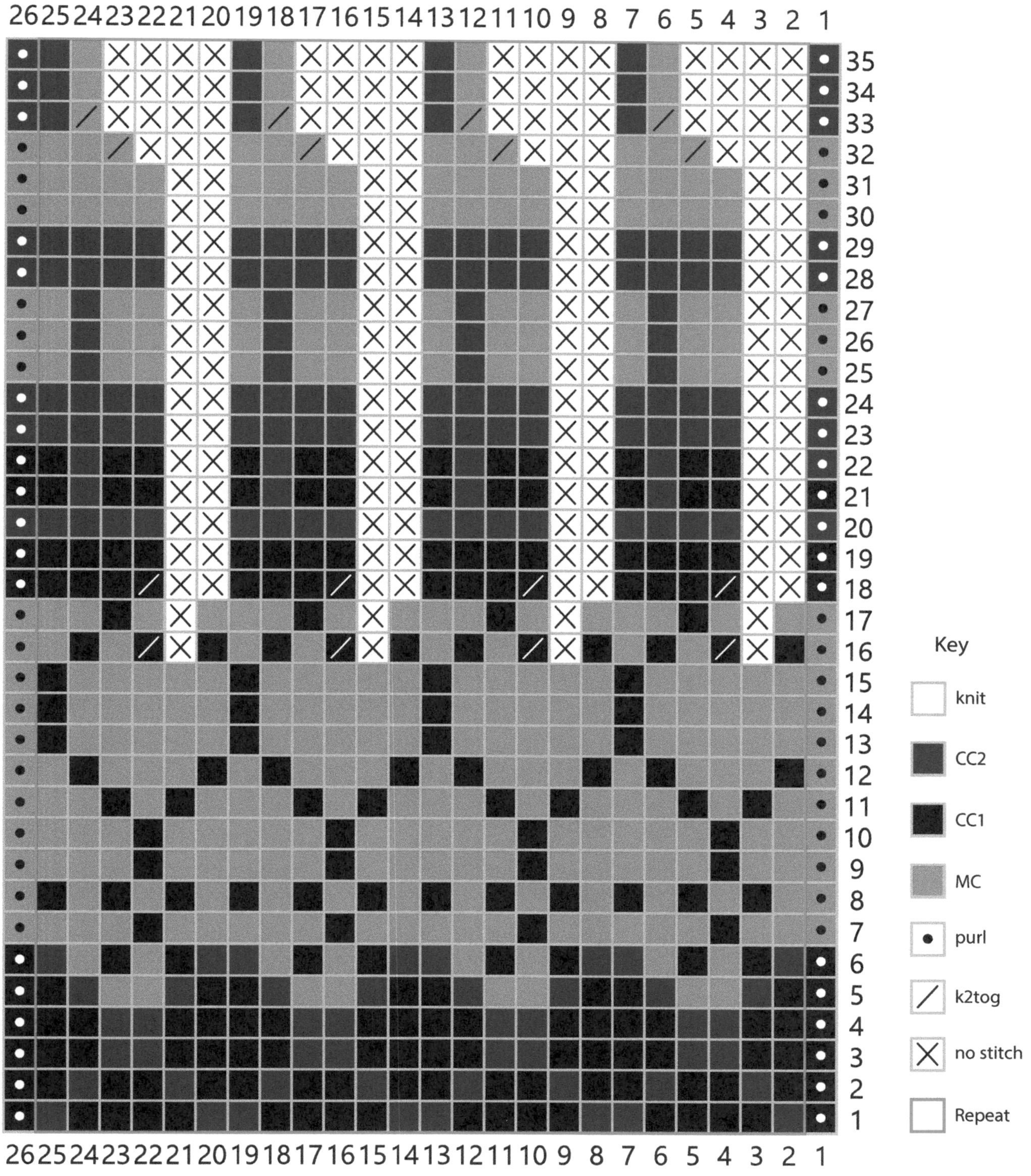

Key

□ knit

■ CC2

■ CC1

■ MC

• purl

╱ k2tog

☒ no stitch

□ Repeat

WAITING CAPE

Named for Agnes Magnúsdóttir, this cape is perfect for stylishly wandering the streets of Reykjavik or brooding near a chilly shore.

Knitting this will be a big departure from everything else you've made in this book! While I love knitting the traditional style of lopapeysa, it's fun to do something a little different with lopi yarn as well. You'll knit from the top down, allowing you to adjust fit as you go, and then work back and forth, joining new balls of yarn for the arm slits.

Difficulty Level
Intermediate

Skills Required
Knit and purl, cast on and bind off
Increasing, decreasing
Working from a chart
Two-color knitting

Materials

YARN
Léttlopi 100% wool; 109 yds/91 m per
1.75 oz/50 g ball)
- MC: #1403 Lapis Blue 9 (9, 11, 11, 12, 12) balls
- CC1: #1700 Air Blue 1 (1, 1, 1, 2, 2) balls

NEEDLES
US size 10/6 mm 32 in/80 cm circular needle
Note: Cape is worked flat. Circular needles are
simply more comfortable for the size of the cape.

NOTIONS
4 stitch markers
2 in/50 mm clasp
Yarn needle
Sewing needle and thread for clasp

Gauge
14 sts/20 rows = 4 in/10 cm square in stockinette
stitch using US 10/6 mm needles

Sizes
XS (S, M, L, XL, 2XL)

Finished Measurements
Width at widest point: 54 (62, 68.5, 75.5, 82.25, 89)
in/137 (157.5, 174, 191.75, 209.5, 226) cm
Neck: 10.25 (12.5, 13.75, 16, 19.5, 21.75) in/26 (31.75,
35, 40.6, 49.5, 55.25) cm
Armhole: 8 in/20.3 cm

Pattern Notes
This cape is meant to be slightly loose and easy
to wear over clothing. If you're in between sizes,
choose one size up, for easy wearing.

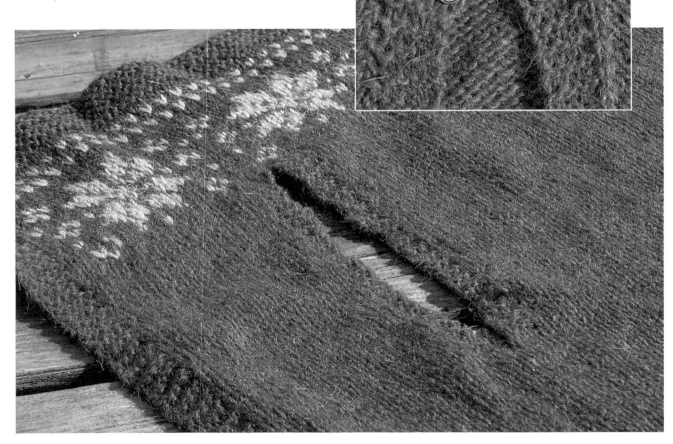

Special Stitches

KF&B
Knit into the front and back of the stitch.

Instructions
Cast on 36 (44, 48, 56, 68, 76) sts.

NECK
Knit 5 rows.

Set up row: K5, pm, k8, pm, k10 (18, 22, 30, 42, 58), pm, k8, pm, k5.

Next row: K5, p to last 5 sts, k5.

Row 1 (inc row): K5, sm, kf&b, k6, kf&b, sm, k to marker, sm, kf&b, k6, kf&b, sm, k5. 40 (48, 52, 60, 72, 80) sts

Row 2: K5, p to last 5 sts, k5.

Next row: K5, sm, kf&b, k to 1 st before marker, kf&b, sm, k to marker, sm, kf&b, k to 1 st before marker, kf&b, sm, k5.

Repeat these two rows until you have 192 (216, 240, 264, 288, 312) sts.

Work in stockinette stitch, maintaining garter st border, until piece measures 23 in/58.4 cm.

ARMHOLES
Knit across one row.

WS: K5, p 20 (24, 28, 28, 32, 32), k3, attach new ball of yarn, k3, p130 (146, 162, 186, 202, 226), k3, attach new ball of yarn, k3, p20 (24, 28, 28, 32, 32), k5.

Next row: Knit across, maintaining armholes.

You can remove increase markers at this point.

Repeat these 2 rows until armhole measures 8 in/20.3 cm.

Next RS row: Knit, increasing 10 sts evenly across 202 (226, 250, 274, 298, 322) sts

Next row (WS): K5, p to last 5 sts, k5.

Note: These 5 sts on either side are part of your border, and not included when working chart.

Begin working from Chart.

Note: I like to place a stitch marker between each chart repeat (every 24 sts).

Work 5 rows garter stitch.

Bind off loosely.

FINISHING
Block, weave in all ends.

Directly below your garter stitch neck, sew a clasp of your choosing. If you would like, you can also sew another clasp 6 in/15 cm down from the first for extra closure.

Waiting Cape Chart

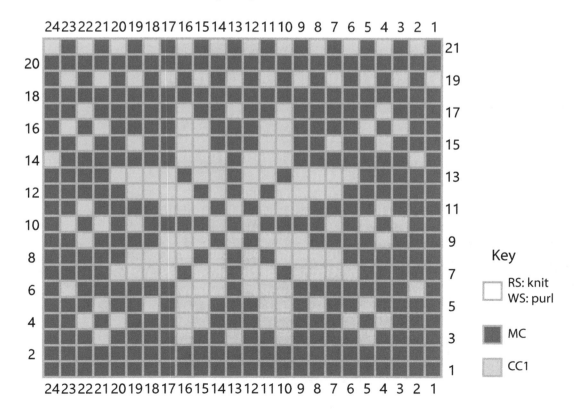

Key

RS: knit
WS: purl

MC

CC1

LEARNED LOPI

Sometimes inspiration just strikes. We were done with this book! Photographs and tech edits were plugging along, and then . . . Iceland happened. As we traveled around, I spied several locals wearing a short-sleeved or sleeveless version of the lopapeysa. When we met Janina, I admired the way she had added rolled edges to her pattern—sometimes beneath a rib edge, sometimes above a purled finished edge. I spied charts that I hadn't seen before. I admired the tufts of grass and random plants or moss that sprouted up on rocky paths to volcanoes and waterfalls. And I found myself grabbing some Léttlopi and swatching . . .

"Are you knitting something new? We leave in three days!" Kyle said. Then he used the network we were amassing in Iceland to find a model. I stayed in our Airbnb in Reykjavik for a solid day and finished the pattern, tried it on, and fell in love.

To me, this shirt represents everything that is Iceland. It is practical. Wear it over a cami on a warm day or over a long-sleeved shirt if it's chilly. It's open to interpretation. Would you like to extend the sleeves all the way down? Easy to do. Want a rib bottom instead of the moss bottom? No problem—it's your recipe, customize it! (By the time this book is published, I'll have finished a dress version of this top by mixing this pattern with the dress pattern on p. 151). It also incorporates some of the things I learned on the trip, such as the rolled edge at the top.

And best of all, it knits up very quickly. As most other items in this book, it's knitted in the round from the bottom up, but when you get to the underarms, you'll knit the front and the back separately, side to side. Then you'll cast on stitches for the shoulders and work in the round again for your yoke. The sleeves are picked up in the round at the end, and again, you can customize as desired by either keeping the sleeve a short cap or extending it down.

Difficulty Level
Intermediate

Skills Required
Knit and purl, cast on and bind off
Increasing, decreasing
Working in the round on circular needles
Working from charts
Stranded colorwork
Picking up stitches

Materials

YARN
Léttlopi (100% wool; 109 yd/100 m per
1.75 oz/50 g ball)
- MC: #1407/Pine Green Heather; 4 (4, 5, 5,
  6, 7) balls
- CC1: #0085/Oatmeal Heather; 1 (2, 2, 3, 3, 4) balls
- CC2: #0867/Chocolate Heather; 1 (1, 1, 2,
  2, 2) balls

NEEDLES
US size 8/5 mm 32 in/80 cm circular needle and
  16 in/40 cm circular needle
US size 8/5 mm dpns or preferred needles for
  working in the round

NOTIONS
2 stitch markers
Stitch holder, waste yarn, or spare circular needle
  for holding front/back stitches
Yarn needle

Gauge
20 sts/24 rounds = 4 in/10 cm
square in stockinette stitch
using US 8/5 mm needles

Sizes
XS (S, M, L, XL, 2XL)

Finished Sizes
Chest: 31 (32, 36, 38, 40, 42) in/78.7 (81.5, 91.5, 96.5,
101.5, 107) cm
Length to underarm: 14 (15, 16, 17, 18, 18) in/35.5 (38,
40.6, 43, 45.7, 45.7) cm

Pattern Notes
This top is worked from the bottom up and is
designed to be a fitted piece with 2 in/5 cm
of negative ease. You can always eliminate the
waist shaping if you would like something less
formfitting.
When working the back-and-forth section at the
underarms, you can try on the top to see if you'd
like a slightly longer/looser armhole.

Special Stitches

MOSS STITCH
Round 1: Knit 1, purl 1 around.
Round 2: Purl 1, knit 1 around.
Repeat rounds 1 and 2 for pattern.

1X1 RIB
Knit 1, purl 1 around.

KF&B
Knit into the front and back of the stitch.

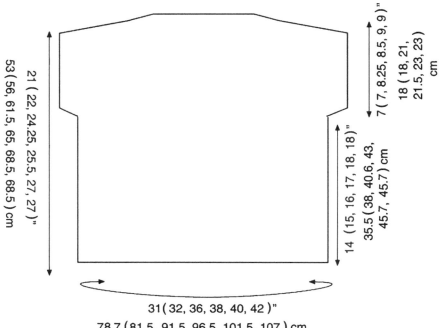

21 (22, 24.25, 25.5, 27, 27)"
53 (56, 61.5, 65, 68.5, 68.5) cm

7 (7, 8.25, 8.5, 9, 9)"
18 (18, 21, 21.5, 23, 23) cm

14 (15, 16, 17, 18, 18)"
35.5 (38, 40.6, 43, 45.7, 45.7) cm

31 (32, 36, 38, 40, 42)"
78.7 (81.5, 91.5, 96.5, 101.5, 107) cm

Instructions

BODY

Using size US 8/5 mm longer circular needle and MC, CO 128 (134, 142, 154, 168, 184) sts.
Pm and join to work in the round.
Work Moss stitch for 6 rounds.
Knit around until piece measures 8 (8.5, 9, 9.25, 9.5, 9.5) in/20 (21, 23, 23.5, 24, 24) cm.

WAIST SHAPING

K64 (67, 71, 77, 84, 92) sts, pm, k to end of round.
Decrease round: K1, ssk, knit to 2 sts before marker, k2tog, sm, k1, ssk, k to last 2 sts, k2tog. 124 (130, 138, 150, 164, 180) sts
Knit 4 rounds.
Repeat these 5 rounds 2 (2, 2, 3, 3, 3) more times. 116 (122, 130, 138, 152, 168) sts.
Increase round: K1, kf&b, knit to 1 st before marker, kf&b, sm, k1, kf&b, knit to 1 st before marker, kf&b. 120 (126, 134, 142, 156, 172) sts
Knit 4 rounds.
Repeat these 5 rounds a total of 3 (3, 3, 4, 4, 4) times. 128 (134, 142, 154, 168, 184) sts
Next round: Inc 1 (0, 0, 1, 1, 1). 129 (134, 142, 155, 169, 185) sts
Knit around until piece measures 14 (15, 16, 17, 18, 18) in/35.5 (38, 40.6, 43, 45.7, 45.7) cm from cast-on edge, or desired length.

UNDERARMS

Knit to 6 (7, 7, 8, 8, 9) sts before marker, BO 12 (14, 14, 16, 16, 18) sts, knit to 6 (7, 7, 8, 8, 9) sts before marker, BO 12 (14, 14, 16, 16, 18) sts.
Begin working back and forth in stockinette stitch until armhole measures 2 (2, 2.25, 2.5, 3, 3) in/5 (5, 5.7, 6.3, 7.5, 7.5) cm ending with a purl row. 105 (106, 114, 123, 137, 149) total sts (both halves)
Place sts on holder or waste yarn and repeat for other side.

YOKE

With MC, CO 41 (46, 53, 54, 58, 63) sts for arm, knit stitches from holder, CO 41 (46, 53, 54, 58, 63) sts for other arm, knit across live stitches, pm. 187 (198, 220, 231, 253, 275) sts
Knit 2 rounds.
Begin working from Chart.
Stitch counts after decrease rounds:
After round 13: 153 (162, 180, 189, 207, 225) sts
After round 19: 119 (126, 140, 147, 161, 175) sts
After round 29: 85 (90, 100, 105, 115, 125) sts
For XS and S, work rounds 1–29 of chart only.

With CC1, purl 2 rounds.
With MC, knit around for 8 rounds.
Bind off loosely.

SLEEVES

With MC and right side facing, pick up and knit 60 (64, 68, 72, 78, 84) sts around armhole using dpns or preferred method for working in the round.
Knit around for 8 rounds.
Work 1x1 rib for 8 rounds.
Bind off in pattern.
Repeat for other sleeve.

FINISHING

Block and weave in ends.

Learned Lopi Chart

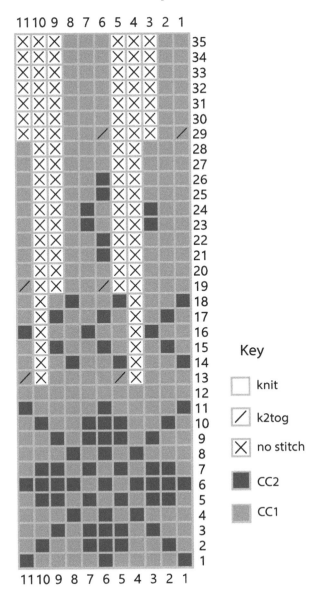

Key

☐	knit
╱	k2tog
☒	no stitch
■	CC2
▨	CC1

VIK DRESS

As a non-Icelander visiting Iceland, I loved seeing the lopapeysa-style dress everywhere we went. Some with short sleeves, some with long. Some dressed up with leggings for a night out, others worn over jeans and boots as a perfectly functional way to beat the cold.

For at least 600 miles of our drive, we kept referring to Janina as "the lady from Vik," but then when we checked our notes in Djupivogur, we realized that we were quite wrong about where she lived, as it wasn't anywhere near Vik. So for the next 150 miles, we jokingly called her "the lady not from Vik." Luckily, it is Iceland, so even though we were wrong about which town she was in, we could still get to her in a short amount of time.

This dress is knit from the bottom up, with decreases and increases to shape the waist.

Difficulty Level
Intermediate

Skills Required
Knit and purl, cast on and bind off
Increasing, decreasing
Working small circumferences in the round on
  dpns/magic loop/two circulars
Stranded knitting
Reading a chart
Grafting

Materials

YARN
Léttlopi (100% wool, 109 yds/100 m per
1.75 oz/50 g)
- MC: #1403/Lapis Blue Heather; 12 (13, 14, 15, 15,
  16, 17) balls
- CC1: #1702/Milkyway; 1 (2, 2, 3, 3, 4, 4) balls
- CC2: #1707 Galaxy; 1 (1, 2, 2, 2, 2, 3) balls

NEEDLES
US size 8/5 mm 24 in/60 cm circular needle
US size 8/5 mm double-pointed needles or
  preferred method for small circumference

NOTIONS
3 stitch markers
6 stitch holders or waste yarn

Gauge
20 sts/24 rounds = 4 in/10 cm square
on US 8/5 mm needles

Sizes
XS (S, M, L, XL, 2XL, 3XL)

Finished Measurements
Chest: 36.75 (40, 43.25, 48, 51.25, 55.25, 59.25)
in/93.3 (101.6, 110, 122, 130, 140.3, 150.5) cm
Length to underarm: 27 (28, 29, 29.5, 30, 31, 31.5)
in/68.5 (71, 73.5, 75, 76, 78.7, 80) cm
Sleeve to underarm: 18.5 (19, 19.5, 20, 20.5, 20.5, 21)
in/47 (48.25, 49.5, 51, 52, 52, 53.5) cm

Pattern Notes
This dress is designed with 2–3 in/5–7.5 cm of
positive ease. Choose a size down from your
regular chest size for a more fitted dress.
This dress is knit from the bottom up with waist
shaping. If you prefer, you can eliminate the waist-
shaping section and just knit it as one tube. You
can also adjust the length of the skirt to make it
longer or shorter, however you wish.

Special Stitches

1X1 RIB
Knit 1, purl 1 around.

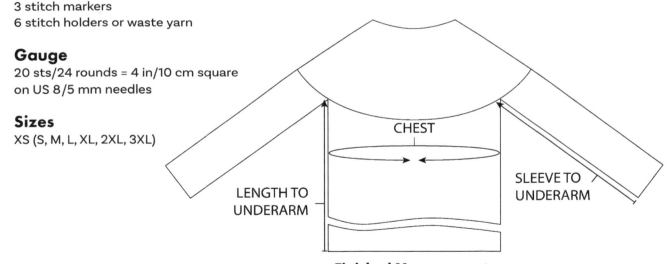

Finished Measurements
XS (S, M, L, XL, 2XL, 3XL)

Chest: 36.75 (40, 43.25, 48, 51.25, 55.25, 59.25)" /
93.34 (101.6, 110, 122, 130, 140.3, 150.5) cm

Length to Underarm: 27 (28, 29, 29.5, 30, 31, 31.5)" /
68.5 (71, 73.5, 75, 76, 78.7, 80) cm

Sleeve to Underarm: 18.5 (19,19.5, 20, 20.5, 20.5, 21)" /
47 (48.25, 49.5, 51, 52, 52, 53) cm

The Vik Dress Chart

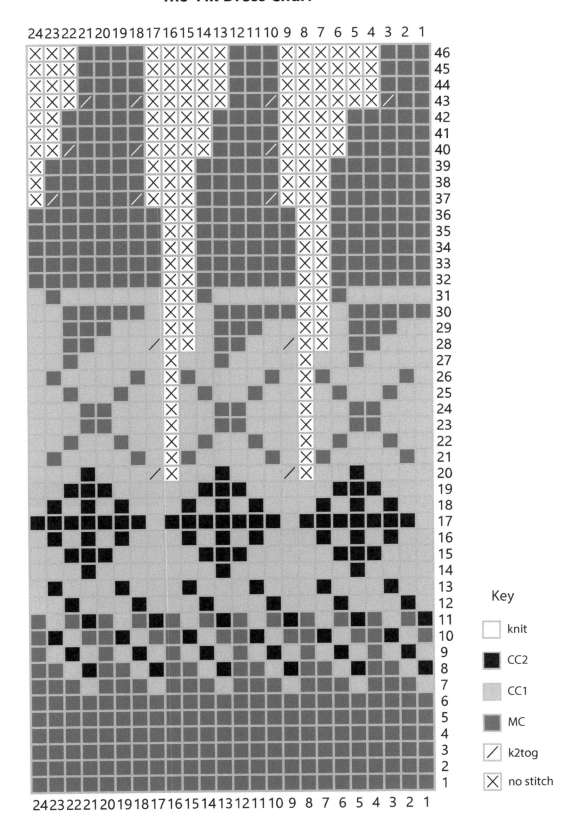

Key

- ☐ knit
- ■ CC2
- ■ CC1
- ■ MC
- ╱ k2tog
- ☒ no stitch

Instructions

BODY

With MC, CO 184 (200, 216, 240, 256, 276, 296) sts.
Place marker and join to work in the round.
Rounds 1–12: Work 1x1 Rib.
Knit around until piece measures 14 (14.5, 15, 15.5, 16, 16.5, 17) in/35.5 (36.8, 38, 39, 40.6, 42, 43) cm from cast-on edge.

WAIST SHAPING

Setup round: K46 (50, 54, 60, 64, 69, 74), pm, k92 (100, 108, 120, 128, 138, 148), pm, k46 (50, 54, 60, 64, 69, 74).
Decrease round: K to 2 sts before marker, k2tog, sm, ssk, k to 2 sts before next marker, k2tog sm, ssk, k to end of round. 180 (196, 212, 236, 252, 272, 292) sts
Knit 2 rounds.
Repeat these 3 rounds 7 (7, 8, 8, 8, 8, 8) more times. 152 (168, 180, 204, 220, 240, 260) sts
Knit around for 12 (14, 14, 16, 16, 18, 18) rounds.
Increase round: K to marker, M1L, sm, k1, M1R, k to next marker, M1L, sm, k1, M1R, k to end. 156 (172, 184, 208, 224, 244, 264) sts
Knit 2 rounds.
Repeat these 3 rounds 7 (7, 8, 8, 8, 8, 8) more times. 184 (200, 216, 240, 256, 276, 296) sts
Remove side markers and knit until piece measures 27 (28, 29, 29.5, 30, 31, 31.5) in/68.5 (71, 73.5, 75, 76, 78.7, 80) cm or desired length.
Set body aside and begin sleeves.

SLEEVES (MAKE 2)
With dpns or preferred method for working in the round cast on 34 (40, 44, 46, 50, 54, 58) sts.
Place marker and join to work in the round.
Work 1x1 Rib for 20 (22, 24, 24, 24, 24, 24) rounds.
Knit around for 2 rounds.
Increase round: K1, m1, k to marker, m1. 36 (42, 46, 48, 52, 56, 60) sts
Knit around for 5 rounds.
Repeat these 6 rounds 7 (8, 8, 9, 10, 11, 11) more times. 50 (58, 62, 66, 72, 78, 82) sts
Knit until sleeve measures 18.5 (19, 19.5, 20, 20.5, 20.5, 21) in/47 (48.25, 49.5, 51, 52, 52, 53.5) cm from cast-on edge.
Place 11 (13, 13, 15, 16, 18, 19) sts on holder for underarm. 39 (45, 49, 51, 56, 60, 63) sts
Place remaining stitches on waste yarn or holder and work other sleeve.

YOKE
Join body and sleeves with MC using circular needle.
K40 (43, 47, 53, 56, 60, 64) sts, place 11 (13, 13, 15, 16, 18, 19) sts from body onto holder for underarm, k39 (45, 49, 51, 56 , 60, 63) sleeve sts, k82 (88, 96, 104, 112, 120, 130) sts across back, place 11 (13, 13, 15, 16, 18, 19) sts from body onto holder for underarm, k39 (45, 49, 51, 56, 60, 63) sleeve sts, k40 (43, 47, 53, 56, 60, 64) sts to end. 240 (264, 288, 312, 336, 360, 384) sts
Begin working from Chart.
For size S, skip rounds 5 and 6.
Work 1x1 Rib around for 6 rounds.
Bind off in pattern.

FINISHING
Graft underarms; weave in all ends.
Block.

Acknowledgments

A book is always a group effort. From researching, to writing, to publication we have relied upon the efforts of many people.

Among them:

Our agent, Gordon Warnock at Fuse Literary, who believed in this book when it was just a vague idea and carried that enthusiasm to Stackpole Books, where our editor, Candi Derr, scooped it up with love and attention.

Our Icelandic traveling companions Alon Abramson and Arwin Thomasson, who circumnavigated the island, won races, and kept not just the spirit of adventure but also the RV going—without them we'd still be trying to get out of the parking lot.

Kristinn Snær Agnarsson, who opened up his Rolodex and introduced us to people across Iceland. Without him this would have been a very different book. Thanks to Amanda Palmer for introducing us.

Eyþór Máni Steinarsson, who was of immeasurable help in Iceland, in translating, guiding, and being an ambassador—all while carrying on his own busy schedule.

Mikael Hannes, for taking so much time to show us around, and whose ability to wear a sweater splendidly we're certain helped to sell this book.

Amy Singer, who was enthusiastic at an early stage and offered help, advice, and alacrity.

Alanna Okun, who shared her joy of knitting and stories with us.

Hjördís Albertsdóttir, for opening the secret caves of Mývatn.

Mary Kinney, for advice and expertise.

Kate Atherley, who shared her power and talent, fame, and good humor.

Charles and Susan Summerfield, who proudly wore Kyle's first knitting projects and pretended they didn't notice gross irregularities in both form and function.

The Philadelphia Drunken Knitwits, who encouraged Kyle on weekly Zoom meetups. Fellow knitters Linda Ruggiero, Sherry Michael, Rebecca Johnson, Laurel Price Gaylor, and David Toccafondi.

Our local knitting stores, Loop and My Stitch Central in Philadelphia.

Thanks to Kristin Vala Breidfjord, president of the Icelandic Handicraft Society, for permission to reprint the photo from Hugur og Hön; to Guðný Dóra, from the Laxness Museum for allowing us to reprint the photograph of Auður Laxness wearing her early lopi; and to Gudmundur Ingolfsson who kindly let us reprint his photograph of the page from Jón Einarsson's Icelandic Sjónabók.

Special thanks to Ásdís Jóelsdóttir and Védís Jónsdóttir, two of the world's leading lopapeysa experts, who took the time to answer our questions. Without their kind help this book would have been much less interesting.

On the Philadelphia front, Brad Hafford and Mike Vanhelder, who kept the home fires burning and the cats fed while we were in Iceland.

On the Indiana front, Dill Her0 and the Strange Brew Crew for keeping the walls up and Evelyn occupied and happy.

Index

Page numbers for photos are *italicized*. Page numbers followed by the letter "n" refer to footnotes.